Much of the story of the German aircrew who defected to the British is still on the 'Closed' files of the Special Intelligence Service – the S.I.S. The Germans are still alive and in hiding from their former comrades. The S.I.S. guards well the secret of the great coup it pulled off which saved innumerable British lives. This is the story of that great coup which, in Winston Churchill's immortal words, 'turned the tide' of the war.

Robert Hill

The Great Coup

CORGI BOOKS
A DIVISION OF TRANSWORLD PUBLISHERS LTD

THE GREAT COUP

A CORGI BOOK 0 552 10959 2

Originally published in Great Britain by
Arlington Books (Publishers) Ltd.

PRINTING HISTORY
Arlington Books edition published 1977
Corgi edition published 1978

This book is set in Intertype Baskerville

Corgi Books are published by
Transworld Publishers Ltd.,
Century House, 61–63 Uxbridge Road,
Ealing, London W5 5SA
Made and printed in Great Britain by
Cox & Wyman Ltd., London, Reading and Fakenham

To C.C. who put the burr under my saddle

Author's Note

Establishing the truth about a series of events which happened as recently as thirty-five years ago inevitably presents some conflicts of opinion. To the British, Schmitt, Rosenberger and Kantwill are heroes. The Germans consider them traitors. There are grey areas in this chronicle of events where I have drawn conclusions from the known facts simply because the files which would provide the answers are still marked 'Closed'.

If those conclusions give offence to anyone still living, or their relatives, I regret it.

Introduction

The least recorded battle of the 1939–45 war is that won by Bomber Command of the R.A.F. The least known commander in the war is the man who won that battle, Marshal of the Royal Air Force Sir Arthur 'Bomber' Harris.

His was the order which sent out the one thousand bombers at a time, to raid the cities of Germany, and for that he was criticised by historians after the war, who claimed that it had little part in the victory.

But, as he pointed out on his eighty-fifth birthday, at a party given in his honour by seven survivors of Bomber Command: It was the raids of Bomber Command which forced Germany to concentrate on building fighter aircraft instead of bombers, and stopped the bombing of Britain. It was the unpredictability of the British raids which forced Germany to divert a million men from the front line, and to convert forty-four thousand anti-tank guns into anti-aircraft guns to protect their cities and factories. It was because Germany had to divert its Air Force to protect their own country, losing command of the air, that after D-Day, thirty-seven Allied divisions, many of them green troops, were able to chase sixty German divisions across Europe and destroy them. It was Bomber Command who won the biggest 'naval battle' by destroying six of Germany's major battleships and a third of their U-boats in their home ports and even factories.

The war cost Bomber Command forty-seven thousand aircrew. But the bomber offensive was described by Hitler's Controller of Armaments, Albert Speer as 'Germany's greatest lost battle, even more devastating than the surrender of the German armies at Stalingrad'. It caused Field

Marshal Erwin Rommel to warn Hitler in 1944, 'Stop the bombers or we cannot win. If we go on, we will simply lose another city every night'.

But Hitler and Goering couldn't. This is the reason why.

CHAPTER ONE

HANS HORST-WESSEL was a Berlin ponce. He died in a brawl with another ponce, over the ownership of a prostitute, in a tavern of Berlin-Weding on the night of February 23rd, 1930. He had also been a friend of Heinrich Himmler, who, soon after the First World War, had also lived off the immoral earnings of women. But now, the two ex-ponces had achieved immortality. One by dying after writing the words to an old German navy tune, which had become the hymn of the Nazi Party. The other by becoming the head of the Gestapo.

It was, Oberleutnant Heinrich Schmitt reflected, a strange world.

The chorus of the Horst-Wessel song, whose stirring tune, spoiled by the nationalistic words of the dead S.A. leader, had set off his train of thought, grew louder as the doors of a bar opened, and a group of German soldiers lurched into the street. They were obviously drunk, they had their arms round each other in the fraternal friendliness of any group of drunks, as they roared the words of the song. As they stumbled towards Schmitt, they stiffened, and one or two of the more sober prepared to disengage and offer a salute, but Schmitt forestalled them. He adopted a less steady gait himself, and deliberately turned his head away, ramming his hands into the pockets of his Luftwaffe uniform. After all, it was Christmas. It *was* 1942, and anyway it was the uniform they would have saluted and not the man wearing it. Schmitt didn't care a great deal for his uniform.

True, it suited him. He was slim and tall, and any German uniform was designed to look best on tall, slim Nordic men, even when hidden by the fur-collared greatcoat that kept out the winter cold of Denmark. He deliberately broke step, forcing himself not to march with the beat set by the drunks roaring out their chorus. He continued to amble through the streets of Aarlborg, on the Danish coast. He knew it well, but from a different angle, from the air, and as he strolled, he tried to place the roads on the aerial map his imagination conjured up for him.

He hadn't realized it, but his feet had been carrying him in a certain direction, and as he turned a corner, he realized where. There it was, the anonymous building, blacked out like every other building in the Danish town, but which, even had there been no blackout, would still have appeared in darkness. The headquarters of the Geheime Staats-Polizei, the home of the Gestapo.

Undoubtedly there would be a file on him in there, perhaps kept next to the file on his father. The Gestapo, it was well known, had files on everybody. Files which followed one around the country, around the Continent even, keeping the local Gestapo head aware of who was in his territory, particularly if there was some doubt about his political allegiance. Schmitt knew that there had been doubt about his own allegiance. Had he not been a prominent and respected member of the Luftwaffe, and of its 10th Fighter Squadron, he and his father would have known the interior of a headquarters like that very well by now. They would certainly have a file on him. One person they wouldn't have a file on, however, was Himmler himself. He had seen to it that the old police records, which dealt with his relationship with a Berlin prostitute Frieda Wagner, who was found murdered in 1920, disappeared. So too had the record of his arrest in Munich later that year, his trial for her murder, and his subsequent acquittal for lack of evidence.

There would be no mention either of his marriage to a former nurse in an abortion clinic who so mistrusted doctors that she became a herbal fanatic, and gave Himmler his passion for mediaeval herbal remedies about which Germany sniggered – quietly and in private.

Although his feet wanted to flag as they carried him past the Gestapo building, Schmitt refused to let them. He remembered reading that every criminal had inside them the desire to surrender, and that experienced policemen standing casually outside a police-station, would often take a passer-by in for questioning for no reason at all, and then get from that passer-by a confession to a crime that had baffled them.

As that thought came to his mind, Schmitt forced himself to control an urge to quicken his step and leave that place behind. He knew that within the shadows someone would be watching his movements. Perhaps it was an old-time policeman with that instinct for a wrongdoer honed to a frightening clarity. If that instinct did exist, and there was some way of perfecting it, the Gestapo would have done so. He turned another corner, leaving the building out of sight, but again he made his footsteps continue the pace he had set. The watcher, if there was a watcher, would be listening for a change of pace that indicated relief at passing the Gestapo building. He wouldn't be safe until he was out of hearing. Schmitt made a mental note never to pass that way again. He had no idea what he might blurt out if he were taken inside that bleak structure and subjected to the treatment which everyone knew took place, but which everyone preferred not to think about.

Once past the Gestapo headquarters, his nerve-ends relaxed their tension. As his breathing steadied again, he realized that the adrenalin had been pumping up, and that he had been feeling as tense as when he took his Junkers 88 up on one of his nightfighter missions. 'Steady,' he told himself wryly. If he was going to live on his nerves as much on the ground as when he was in the air, the strain would begin to show, and that could be fatal to his entire enterprise, if it were noticed by the station medical officer.

He looked about him. He could recognize none of the streets. He was lost, but it didn't matter, Aarlborg, though the fourth largest city in Denmark wasn't *that* big, and though its resistance was active, and was becoming more so, he had no fear of being attacked in the open streets. There were too many German patrols about for that. And anyway, it was Christmas, and the Danes had a greater feeling for that religious festival than the Germans.

Thoughts of Christmas brought memories of his own childhood Christmases. For him, they had been good. He wondered, as he passed the silent houses, dark and seemingly empty, whether behind those doors which few Germans

13

entered without first kicking them down, and poking the barrel of a Schmeisser in, young Danish children would be having the quiet, carefree, innocent Christmas that he once had. He feared not. He and the rest of his country had seen to that. But there was no longer the apathy and hopelessness on the faces of the Danes that he did meet. Instead, behind the impassive expressions they were careful to wear when in the presence of a member of the Wehrmacht, he could read the look of triumph. They knew their time was coming, and that it was now only a question of surviving until that day came. They were prepared to put themselves in limbo until then, endure the days one by one until the Allies freed them, and then forget as quickly as possible the intervening period.

Oberleutnant Schmitt knew exactly how they felt. For he too was in limbo, waiting for the day when he would also be free, and able to forget the events of the past seven years.

His eyes were used to the dark, and he could see better than most, no matter how black the night around him. He had been trained to do so, as all nightfighters were. It had served him and his crew well on their constant missions against the British bombers. It had sufficed to keep him out of their way.

He found himself on the main street of Aarlborg, where, he knew, a bar catering for German officers and the few collaborators among the Danes, would still be open. More important, it had a telephone on a wall, where a whispered conversation would not be overheard. Once inside, he hung up his cap and greatcoat and took a quiet look around. At the bar, drinking the inevitable aquavit were two officers from his own station, who nodded in a friendly fashion to Schmitt as he took stock of his surroundings. Schmitt smiled back at them, and accepted their unspoken invitation to join their group.

'Good weather for flying,' said one, as he gestured to the barman and another glass of the cold, potent liquor was poured. Very much like schnapps, thought Schmitt as he clicked his heels, raised his glass in the toast 'Prosit', and emptied it of its contents, reaching almost automatically for the glass of lager which had appeared on the bar, to chase it down. He fought down the urge to cough, and controlled the muscles of his throat as they contracted in reaction to the

14

spirit. He made a point of drinking seldom, if at all, without making it too obvious that he didn't drink. People in drink talk, and Schmitt had much to say that mustn't be said.

'Lovely weather,' he agreed. Each knew what the other meant. There was little chance in the weather conditions outside of any fighter taking off, let alone seeking out bombers. The cloud seemed to stretch from the ground to eternity. But for Schmitt, the other pilots of 10th Squadron, and for the rest of the Group, it was lovely weather. Much too bad for the British bombers to fly, which meant that the nightfighters, at last, could have a brief rest. Since the night of May 30th, 1942, when the British bomber commander, Air Chief Marshal Harris, had silenced the criticism of the Army and Navy Chiefs of Staff by launching his first 'One Thousand bomber' raids on Cologne, the nightfighters of the Luftwaffe had enjoyed little rest. Now, even single nights on the ground offered precious moments in which to relax, and get drunk.

Schmitt signalled for the next round. The telephone he noticed, was not being used. He excused himself as the drinks were served, and went towards it. The others at the bar nodded knowingly. Schmitt, they had all long ago concluded, was an odd character, who kept himself very much to himself. Perhaps this was the reason why. He had his own 'contacts' in Aarlborg.

They were right.

He heard the 'click' as the receiver was lifted, but no voice answered. Schmitt uttered one brief sentence and replaced the receiver. If any member of the Abfehr *were* listening in to the conversation from the bar, the address would give them little information. If they searched it even, they would not know what they were looking for. There was a certain amount of risk attached to making the call, as it was made in front of the barman and the other officers, and a simple enquiry would establish that the call was made by Schmitt. But, there was no real reason why the phone should be tapped, and making the call from there was much safer than using a phone on the station, where most outgoing calls were automatically monitored, or from any other civilian phone. And it was infinitely preferable to passing on the information he had to give by hand.

15

The night was still young, but the other two pilots were becoming restive. The time-clocks which the past few months had built into their metabolic system were registering action-time, the time when they would normally either be strapped into the cockpits of their aircraft, or standing by in the dispersal room of the base, waiting for the 'Achtung' call to come over the Tannoy. And though they were technically stood down for the night, the instinct in them was to return to the airfield, just in case. Tired, drained though they were, they were still members of the Luftwaffe, once the finest air force the world had known. They moved towards the coat-rack, and Schmitt, leaving his own drinks on the bar, went with them. He didn't want the alcohol, and now that he had completed his mission, there was no reason for him to hang around the city. He might as well take a lift back with them. He too could show enthusiasm. He had been feigning it long enough.

In England, 'Bomber' Harris was fighting an action on two fronts, the offensive against the Axis, and a defensive one against the critics who wanted Bomber Command disbanded, and the planes and crews attached to the Army and Navy as a tactical force. The morale of the crews flying the bombers was low. The German defensive system, of anti-aircraft guns and nightfighters, was making each bombing mission a suicide one for a large proportion of the bomber fleets. He had managed to fend off the critics with the thousand bomber raids on first Cologne, then Essen and then Bremen, even though it had meant putting into the air virtually every aircraft that could possibly fly; even though some of them had no chance of reaching the target.

The raids captured the imagination of the public, and their positive reaction was caught by the bomber crews. Morale lifted, but it was still lower than Harris thought healthy, and the results of the raids over Germany were still not good enough for his high standards. But while the morale of Bomber Command was low, that of the Luftwaffe night-fighters was high. It was the morale of the German High Command that was low. The aircrews thought they were winning the battle. The High Command knew they were not. They had realized that while the British and American air forces were improving the quality and performance of their bombers and fighters, and were building them in ever-increasing numbers, the German Air Force had committed itself to building bombers, which it was no longer able to use, and to the fighters with which it had commenced the war. Although the aircraft factories of Messerschmitt and Junkers were desperately trying to provide more powerful engines for these aircraft, to equal the performance of the British fighters, they continued to lag behind.

Schmitt was one of the few who realized that, if the British Bomber Command could keep up its attacks, the Luftwaffe would wear out more quickly than anyone thought.

He, with Adolf Galland, Werner Baumbach, Lutzow, Oesau, Pelz and a dozen more, were all that remained of the products of the Air Warfare School, at Gatow, Berlin, the first of the cadet classes of the young German Luftwaffe. Thousands had applied, only a few hundred had been accepted, for the course which Hermann Goering had established in 1936. The aircraft industry had equipped them with the finest fighters and bombers of any air force. In 1939, while the R.A.F. was composed of three thousand six hundred front-line aircraft, only twenty per cent of them first class, with no more than five hundred first-line bombers and two hundred first-line fighters, the Luftwaffe showed a different picture.

They could fly one thousand one hundred and eighty medium bombers, seven hundred and seventy-one single-seat fighters; three hundred and thirty-six dive bombers, and four hundred and eight attack wings of Me 110 and Me 109 aircraft.

They were good aircraft then, but they were now rapidly becoming obsolescent, and they were still being flown by the Luftwaffe.

In the mess at Aarlborg aerodrome, the smiles of the other pilots as they bought each other drinks at the bar, and the cheeriness of the mess waiters as they served drinks at the tables confirmed what they already knew from the mist and drizzle outside. It was a non-flying night. The raiders hadn't come.

CHAPTER TWO

HEINRICH SCHMITT was one of the few people on the Continent to know what was happening in his own country, and those which Germany had occupied. Germany and Britain were at war, but there were still routes linking the two countries, and if a Luftwaffe pilot was determined, and curious enough to take the risk, there was much that he could learn. Schmitt was determined and curious, but it brought him information which he wished he had never learned.

He knew about the methods of the S.S. and the Gestapo. He knew that, even at that time, thousands of people guilty of no greater offence than expressing doubt about the possibility of Germany winning the war, even though they were homeless as a result of British and American bombing attacks, were being arrested and jammed into the Gestapo cells at Alexanderplatz in Berlin. And he knew that with one slip, he could so easily join them in those same cells. For only a brief time before he had become the subject of the Gestapo's very serious attentions which would end only with a pistol or concentration camp.

But he also knew of the gradual resistance to Hitler and the Nazi Party which was building up in Germany, for he was helping to foster it. Already in the cities which had been the targets for the raids of retribution by Bomber Command, the Gestapo had tightened its grip on the civilian population. A group of women who had answered an advertisement inserted in a newspaper by the owner of a bomb-damaged chemist offering cosmetics in a sale between the hours of two and four in the afternoon, formed a queue long before the sale started. All had their names taken by the Gestapo in one of their swoops and found themselves peeling potatoes for six hours in an Army kitchen. The Gestapo told them that if they had time to spare to queue for such frivolous items as make-up, they could spend it more usefully.

The same explanation was given to any woman who walked about looking reasonably smart even though she was wearing clothes bought long before the war, or some of the loot sent back by her man at the front. She was almost certain to be stopped by the police, asked what war-work she was doing, and stripped of her finery at the police headquarters. There were few smart looking women in Germany as a result.

The bombing had resulted in an accommodation problem, and tenants of the flats and houses that survived were forced to live in one of their rooms, while each of the others was occupied by four people.

But almost as fast as the Allies destroyed, the slave battalions of the occupied countries rebuilt. Labour was cheap. The Nazis were using every ounce of it, for already, though the war had two more years to run, they knew that it was as good as lost, and their slogan was ' Have as good a time as you can during the war. The peace will be frightful.' Germany and the Nazis had nowhere to go except down, and they were determined to take as many people as they could down with them.

For certain of the Nazi leaders there was an opportunity for a breathing space – in neutral Sweden. There was a regular rest and recuperation route flown by Luftwaffe pilots, taking high-ranking Nazis for week-ends away from the war, ostensibly on some Government business or other. People like the Nazi Press chief, Paul Schmidt, even had mistresses in Sweden whom they visited regularly. The pilots of those transport aircraft enjoyed the same privileges as the men they flew. Not for them the harrowing nights spent chasing British bombers, and eluding British fighters. They were under strict orders to select the safest routes across the Continent, and they never flew if there was a chance that British or American fighters would be in the air. They were going to survive the war, and many of them had confessed to Schmitt that they had already established homes and identities in Stockholm ready for the end. Their only problem was to decide when that end would be, and which of the flights they took should be the one way journey. In the meantime, like their passengers, they secreted as much money and loot as they could aboard their aircraft, converting it into Swedish currency, and depositing it in a Swedish bank under the name they would one day adopt. The links with Sweden were very strong. Hadn't Goering, the leader of the Luftwaffe, got a Swedish wife?

Schmitt nodded sympathetically as he heard these stories from the pilots, the Flying Chauffeurs of the Nazi chiefs. Their confidencies were safe with him, though they wouldn't have been with all the pilots on his station. The fighter pilots treated these colleagues with disdain, just as every fighting man did those who had the fortune to fight a war from the comfort of a headquarters. The transport pilots felt themselves inferior, and while not prepared to take the risk of a transfer to more active flying duties, wanted to justify themselves to real fliers. Schmitt was always ready to lend them his ear. Much could be learned from them which could be useful elsewhere. And anyway, he felt an affinity with them. He had made his own contingency plans, and they didn't include dying for the Fatherland.

His plans needed care too. The strain of his double life became greater with each day, and with each mission he flew. Despite all his efforts to avoid combat with the Allied bombers, and at the same time appear to be the intrepid pilot his squadron thought him, there was always the risk that he would allow himself to be caught within the range of a British air-gunner's machine guns.

The greater risk came when, again empty-handed, he returned to base, to report once again his lack of success. Fortunately, the German de-briefing system was nowhere near as efficient as that of the R.A.F. All that the intelligence officer was interested in was the number of 'kills' achieved by each pilot. That was the figure that mattered to each head-quarters, and ultimately to Goering and Hitler. Schmitt's own individual lack of success became lost in the triumph of the squadron. The 10th was an 'ace' squadron, the fact that one of its members had the worst luck of the Luftwaffe was known to few. But it *was* known to those on the station, and those who knew included the resident Gestapo officer, responsible for party discipline. He it was that Schmitt feared.

He told himself that it was imagination that caused him to think the gentle conversations that the Gestapo man seemed to like holding with him were more than an eagerness to learn of the life of a fighter pilot. Schmitt's colleagues treated the man in the black uniform with a cold disdain. Heinrich Schmitt found it difficult to do so. He didn't want to encourage the man's approaches, but he found it difficult to use the contemptuous attitude of the others. And once having placed himself in the role of the anxious listener, as the man from the Geheime Staats-Polizei began telling him of his troubles and his problems, he found it impossible to snub him.

Having opened his own heart, the Gestapo man invited confidences in return. Schmitt guarded his tongue, and began to avoid the mess as much as possible, the only common meeting ground. Fortunately, he had never been a regular participant in the aircrews' hi-jinks whenever they were off flying. His absence wasn't too conspicuous, but he had begun to wonder whether it *was* imagination, or whether there really was a speculative look in the Gestapo man's eyes on the occasions they met on the station. *Was* it coincidence, or did he see the man more frequently now? Could it be that he *was* being kept under gentle observation?

Schmitt began noticing the condition he left his room, after his servant had cleaned it up. But when he found himself wanting to return to his billet to check whether anything *had* been disturbed he forced himself to take a cold control. If it was a war of nerves – and he knew that the Gestapo could fight that war better than anybody – he was in danger of losing, of giving himself away by out of character behaviour. Any strange actions now might not only cause greater interest to be taken by the Gestapo, but it could cause his flight and squadron commanders to have doubt in his flying abilities. To be grounded was not only the ultimate indignity for a Luftwaffe fighter pilot, particularly when pilots were so short that half trained youths were being sent up against the bombers, it would also ruin the plans he had begun laying so carefully.

It wouldn't need much however, for the ace who commanded his squadron to drop Schmitt from the flight list. Many of the half-trained youths had been more successful than he, though their active flying had been limited, curtailed by their own inexperience and the British guns. But still they had scored successes.

Nevertheless, Schmitt knew that he would have to take

21

some action soon or else he would crack. It was time to consult his wireless operator, Paul Rosenberger, and put their plan into operation. And it was time to send another signal through the grapevine stretching across Europe and through the neutral countries. It was time to get out, and make his biggest contribution towards ending the war. It was time for his *Great Coup*.

CHAPTER THREE

It was a Sunday. In May. But that north-east corner of the British Isles known as the 'Broch' pays little attention to the months of the calendar. It should have been spring, but instead, rain and gales were sweeping the fishing ports of Peterhead, Fraserburgh and Buckie. The Seine-netters and drifters of the Scottish fishing fleets were tied up in their harbours, and at R.A.F. Dyce the two Spitfire VBs of the duty flight were being kept warm by their ground crews. Their two pilots, Flight Lieutenant A. F. Roscoe, D.F.C., an American who had formerly belonged to the Eagle Squadron, and Sergeant B. R. Scaman, a Canadian, played an interminable game of draughts in the dispersal room.

Meanwhile, at Aarlborg, a Luftwaffe nightfighter airfield in Denmark, Oberleutnant Heinrich Schmitt took a last look around the small room, which with others like it, had been his home since the days he flew with the Condor Legion in the Spanish Civil War. The feeling this time was slightly different, every other time he had taken his Ju 88 nightfighter up, there was always the chance that he wouldn't be coming back to his little cell. But this time, it wasn't a matter of chance. It was a certainty.

He toyed with the few personal effects on the locker beside his bed. He had never been a person for souvenirs. They gave too much personality away, and Schmitt preferred to be thought the distant aesthete. There was the photograph of his father. He picked it up, he would have liked to take it with him, and half moved his hand to drop it in the pocket of his flying overalls, but discretion decided otherwise. The cigarette case, given to him as a present, how long ago, he could hardly remember. That, he placed in a drawer. Perhaps, one day, after his few personal effects had been posted on to his father, he might catch up with it again. True, he wouldn't be coming back from this flight, so it didn't matter if the Gestapo snooper *did* notice they were gone, but it would be better to keep the mystery going as long as possible. Taking the few things which would be remembered as having stood beside his bed would only raise suspicions.

Schmitt took one last look round, opened the door of his billet, and without another glance back, left.

Outside, waiting for him, were his crew. Oberfeldwebel Paul Rosenberger, his wireless operator, and Oberfeldwebel Erich Kantwill, his mechanic. Rosenberger looked calm, but then he always did. He had grown used to living on the edge of a volcano, that was liable to erupt into the shape of a Gestapo man at any time. Kantwill wore the hunted look that had become a part of him since the day he had been posted to Schmitt's plane. They took their usual seats in the Volkswagen utility, and let the driver take them to their plane.

Schmitt, as usual, was urbane. He turned round to his mechanic, and for the sake of the driver, patted his hand. 'Don't worry. Nothing to worry about on this flight. I'll get you back.'

It was, as he well knew, the least of Kantwill's worries. No-one doubted that Heinrich Schmitt would bring his plane and his crew back to base. He was one of the Luftwaffe's best fliers, and had been known to bring a shot-up fighter back when lesser pilots would long since have baled out, and gone into a British prisoner of war camp, or worse, the drink. But he said nothing as they got out of the truck, and walked the few yards to their plane. Its engines had also been kept warm by the mechanics, though, unlike their British counterparts, the aircraft weren't left out in the open, but kept in snug, warm hangars. The two radial, B.M.W. 801 motors, air-cooled, which gave the plane a better performance than its British counterpart the Beaufighter, and an endurance of eight hours flying, were in peak condition.

Though it was only early afternoon, like Dyce, the light was poor as the three men climbed into the cramped cockpit of the Junkers. The date : May 9th, 1943. Britain and the Allies had been at war with Germany for four years, and at last, the tide had begun to turn for the Allies. Those who studied events knew that Germany was losing, but there was still plenty of life left in the German war machines, life like Junkers 88 C-6/R-1, number D5-EV, an all-black nightfighter of the Luftwaffe's 10th nightfighter squadron ... one of the first twelve Junkers nightfighters to be equipped with Air Interception equipment, airborne radar, which enabled them to seek out the British bombers at night, no matter what the conditions were like. The device that enabled them to cut through night, low-cloud and even fog. The Lichtenstein radar.

Schmitt let the other two climb into the plane before following them and settling himself into the left-hand pilot's seat. He caught the signal from the mechanic operating the portable accumulator plugged into his starboard engine, and pressed the starter motor for it. The propeller spun once, twice, three times before it caught. The port engine was warmer. It needed no more than one turn with the booster battery before Schmitt caught it with the throttle. He revved both engines up before allowing them to idle, while he fastened his own straps. The flight mechanic leant over the cockpit, and helped him on with them. Before dropping down off the wing, he shouted something to Schmitt, but whatever it was vanished in the noise of the engines. Schmitt nodded back and smiled. It was probably an exhortation to whatever God he prayed to, perhaps even the Fuhrer himself, to break the cursed luck which had dogged Schmitt throughout his entire career as a fighter pilot.

Although recognized as one of Germany's greatest nightfighter pilots, and with an Iron Cross 1st class to his credit, he had never shot down a single British airplane.

In the dispersal room at Dyce, the two pilots of the Blue flight were waiting to hear the six o'clock news. Things were looking better. General Montgomery had beaten Rommel in the North African campaign, and the Eighth Army was victorious. The Russian armies were pushing the Germans back, and the big raids on German industrial cities had begun – but at a cost. The casualty figures were mounting, and with each report on the B.B.C. news of another raid on the heart of Germany, the number of Lancasters, Stirling and Halifax bombers that failed to return grew. The Germans' own ground-radar system, and its newly fitted Lichtenstein air-radar was becoming more and more effective.

Schmitt circled Aarlborg to gain height and then set

course for Kristiansand to refuel. It was a normal flight, normal practice. With the maximum amount of fuel on board he was on a special mission, not to attack the bombing fleets which nightly, when weather permitted, droned their way across the North Sea, over Denmark and Holland on their way to the Ruhr, but to shoot down specific targets; unarmed, but fast Mosquitos which conveyed couriers and mail from Britain to neutral Sweden.

His orders were specific. A particular plane which would be at a certain map reference at a certain time was to be ignored. Instead, he was to attack the one that followed. Schmitt recognized the order for what it was as soon as he was given the mission. It was a trial. If he couldn't shoot down unsuspecting bombers, even though they had the guns to fire back, perhaps he would have more luck with the unarmed Mosquitos.

At first his failure to score had been a Squadron joke. But as year succeeded year, and still one of the best pilots in the Luftwaffe failed to carry a single R.A.F. roundel on the fuselage of his Junkers, his record ceased to be funny. And now, he and Rosenberger knew that suspicion had replaced it. He could tell it by the way others stopped talking about their successes in the mess. With their Lichtenstein equipment, they were saying, they couldn't fail against the Tommies. It was like shooting sitting ducks. What was wrong with Schmitt that he couldn't join in the bonanza?

Only his record had saved him from more than a mild admonishment and surprise from his commanding officer, Hauptmann Kratz, the 10th Squadron C.O. His courage *had* been unquestioned. Hadn't he been one of the bomber crews in the Condor Legion which had razed Guernica, the defenceless Spanish town made famous by Picasso? Had he not been a test pilot of the Ju 86, the Heinkel 111 and the Dornier 17 during the Civil War? Afterwards, he had transferred to fighters and had become one of the best nightfighter pilots in the Luftwaffe. But he was still unblooded, despite being one of the twelve pilots, handpicked to be entrusted with Goering's answer to the British bomber attacks – the radar-equipped nightfighters.

Other pilots were setting up records of kills. Schmitt had still to open his account.

If he didn't score on this flight, and returned to his base, Schmitt knew that he would be grounded and his plane handed over to someone prepared either to kill or be killed. After that there would probably be questions asked, and almost certainly Erich Kantwill would be persuaded to talk about the times he had implored his pilot to shoot. There had been many times when the big fat fuselages of Lancasters and Halifaxes had loomed large in front of the split perspex windscreen. Large enough even for Kantwill at the rear of the cockpit to know that a certain kill had presented itself and been ignored.

With Kantwill's testimony triggering off doubt into suspicion, reference to his flying logbooks during the Battle of Britain would seal his fate. There they were recorded. An impressive number of attacks on R.A.F. planes, some of them even slow, lumbering biplanes, most of them poorly armed and ineffectual against Schmitt's fighter, in the early days of the Battle. But, curiously enough while he pressed his attacks home, as his fellow pilots corroborated, his bullets never shot an enemy down.

With his Lichtenstein radar, four long toasting-fork aerials projecting from the nose of his fighter, Schmitt now had no excuse for not scoring. He had used up every possible explanation. Back in Germany, and in the occupied countries, the rush was on to equip squadrons of Junkers and Me 110s, four hundred of them, with the device. And once they were fitted, the R.A.F. bombers would be at the mercy of the Luftwaffe.

Heinrich Schmitt, fighter-ace extraordinary knew that, and so did the two N.C.O.s who made up his crew, Rosenberger and Kantwill.

Below them, the Danish coast slipped away to be replaced by the grey emptiness of the North Sea. Schmitt moved the controls a fraction, and the nose of the aircraft eased a few more points to the West. Behind him, on the canvas seat where he looked after the three Oerlikon 20mm cannon which were the aircraft's main armament, Erich Kantwill fidgeted. He coughed into the intercom of his flying helmet, but before he could speak, Rosenberger sitting beside Schmitt half-turned and waved him to silence.

The unsynchronized engines which gave all German aircraft that characteristic half-echo sound churned on.

27

Rosenberger was busy with his calculations. He nudged Schmitt, and as the pilot turned, gestured downwards. Schmitt nodded and pushed the control column forward. The nose of the plane dropped until it was no more than one hundred feet above the North Sea. Schmitt eased the column back and kept his eye on the altimeter, paralleling the cold water. Ahead was Scotland, behind was their base in Norway, the 10th Squadron of Night Fighter Wing No. 3 – the fighter force on which Reichmarshall Goering hoped to recoup his shattered reputation.

Rosenberger took a look at his watch. In Britain it was five thirty, time for tea, thin and watery, but still tea. The Sunday dinner on which most Britons blew their meat ration for the week had long been digested. In Aberdeen, the baps and butties were being toasted.

Kantwill was still trying to make up his mind whether to take some sort of action or not. His hand toyed with the zip of his flying overalls. He could feel the bulk of his pistol in its holster underneath. Would he be able to undo the zip, and draw the gun without the others noticing? But then what? Would he be able to force his senior officer into continuing his mission, or fly back to base?

It hardly needed Schmitt to turn round and read the thoughts going through the man's mind before Kantwill let his hand drop away. For good or ill, he was now committed.

The pencil line that Rosenberger was tracing on his chart moved into square 88/41. He tuned his radio. The time was five forty. He didn't have to force excitement into his voice, it was there already, but he gave it a touch of panic as he broadcast back to his base 'S O S ... S O S ... engine on fire ... we're going to try and land on water ...'

He put the transmitter key off and waited. The reply came almost immediately from his base back in Denmark, promising immediate help and asking for a position. Rosenberger switched the receiver off too. The link with their homeland had been irrevocably broken. He turned round to look expectantly at Kantwill, who fumbled under the seats for three bulky, rubberized packages. He opened one of the windows of the cockpit, and as the howling wind came in from the slipstream, shoved them out into space. The plane carried on, too fast and too low for any of them to observe what happened to the packages. Behind them, on the water of the North Sea, three rubber dinghies unfolded into shape and bobbed about on the water behind them.

At Grove, the Headquarters of Raumstab 100, which controlled the seventeen nightfighter boxes in Denmark, Oberstleutnant von der Pongartz, a fighter pilot of World War I, issued an order. A black cross with the number D5-EV was placed in map reference 88/41. He had already sent out the first patrol to look for the ditched plane and its crew. He was to send a second before he abandoned hope. The dinghies were found, but the plane which spotted them could see there were no occupants, so there was no point sending out a rescue boat just to recover the dinghies. Von der Pongartz began composing the letters of condolence which he would have to send to the relatives of the three men.

Schmitt and Rosenberger weren't worried about them. Only Kantwill was gloomy, even though he had half-prepared his wife not to take too much notice if he failed to return from a mission.

The pencil line that Rosenberger was drawing lengthened until it almost touched the coast of Scotland. He touched Schmitt on the shoulder. The pilot nodded understandingly, and eased back the control column of the Junkers. This was the real danger point. They were encroaching on the preserves of the R.A.F. who were notoriously touchy about airplanes bearing black crosses and Swastikas on their tails. Rosenberger drew the Verey* pistol and made sure that a supply of red-flare cartridges was near at hand.

At five hundred feet Schmitt levelled out the Junkers, and at that precise moment, its blip showed on the British radar defence screens.

The message was flashed to Dyce, and the two duty pilots came out of their reverie.

SCRAMBLE.

* See pp. 34, 98.

CHAPTER FOUR

THERE had been bombing attacks on Aberdeenshire. They didn't compare with the Blitzkriegs upon London and Coventry, and the eventual retaliation upon Hamburg and Dresden, but one had been serious enough upon Aberdeen itself for the anti-aircraft batteries to be brought back, and for 165 Squadron to be posted to Dyce, normally an Operational Training Unit. It gave the football and cricket teams a wider catchment area from which to select their members.

At Dyce, attention was largely concerned with the training for the Inter-flight and section knock-out Football Competition, due to take place on May 19th, when international football referee Peter Craigmyle would take charge of the game between the Maintenance Flight and Station Headquarters.

It was won by the Maintenance Section, and their captain was presented with a cup donated by the officer of the airfield to mark their 8–1 victory.

Before the cricket season started, the Station football team played their sister unit at R.A.F. Peterhead, in aid of the 'Wings for Victory' campaign, and drew two each. That awkward changeover from football to cricket went smoothly, and the Station cricket team competing in the Aberdeen Cricket League, was having a successful start to the season, winning three out of its first four games, and heading the League table. At an Inter-Services athletics meeting at the Linksfield Stadium, Aberdeen, the Station's athletics team came second out of the six competing teams.

Exercising the mind was not forgotten either. There were talks on current affairs, spearheaded by Professor A. C. Hendry and Mr. Fraser McKenzie, while the W.A.A.F.s on the station were lectured on Scottish Castles and Experiences in South America.

The British servicemen and women had a great capacity for grinning and bearing it.

30

For Flight Lieutenant Roscoe, the American, and Sergeant Scaman, the Canadian, the British devotion to football and cricket were strange. On Sunday, May 9th, 1943, the weather outside was continuous heavy rain turning to sleet and snow. There was absolutely *no* incentive to change into shorts and jerseys to kick a ball about on the football pitch. Even the cricket captain had admitted that it was more than a passing shower, unlikely to go away soon and give the team a chance at the nets.

The Met Officer reported ten-tenths cloud at eight hundred feet, clearing to a trace at two thousand five hundred feet. The wind was gale force from the North, north-north-east, which later backed to north-north-west west-north-west and fell away to a slight breeze.

Roscoe and Scaman were content to stay in the dispersal hut with their game of draughts, interspersed with an occasional game of poker. There was no chance of their being called out to fly.

But even though it was Sunday, Aircraftman A. C. Lister from Liverpool, and the rest of B Flight were taking no chances. He was one of five men on duty, keeping the two duty Spitfires in a state of readiness. The starter batteries from the mobile accumulators were plugged in, and the oxygen which the pilots would need when they got airborne was turned on. Everything was ready for a Scramble signal.

It came a few seconds after five thirty, when the Junkers lifted itself into radar range, and the nearest R.A.F. unit was sent up to intercept.

Some days are good for flying. This wasn't. All over Europe, including the Low Countries and Northern France, the weather was squally, with gales in most places, cloudy and frequent thundery showers. The British Bomber Command were still carrying out their anti-submarine missions. One Whitley from St. Eval spotted a U-boat one hundred and thirty-seven miles N.W. of Cap Finisterre, dropped a stick of five Torpex depth charges as it submerged, and then eight minutes later, machine-gunned another sub it caught on the surface five miles farther on. Two Mosquitos were sent out on a weather reconnaissance – but only one returned, the other being posted as missing. That night, twenty-one Stirlings were sent to mine the sea off the west coast of France.

31

And Flight Lieutenant Roscoe was scrambled with Sergeant Scaman to intercept a Ju 88 which had made landfall off Aberdeen.

Roscoe, the former Eagle Squadron pilot, had been in Dyce less than a month. He was the new commander of B Flight, and within days of his arrival, his wingman Scaman had written off a Spitfire when he crash-landed it in a field only two miles from his base. Roscoe's last words as they raced for their aircraft were to take it easy. Although expensive, Spitfires *could* be replaced. Trained pilots were a different matter.

The five duty mechanics already had the engines running on the two planes as Roscoe and Scaman reached them, and as the two pilots climbed aboard, the mechanics left the seats and helped strap the fliers in. The green light flashed in the control tower, and with the flight leader in front, the planes took off. It still wasn't very good flying weather, although the gale was dying out.

At Peterhead, Oberleutnant Schmitt turned his aircraft south down the coast towards Aberdeen and waited for the escort he knew must come. Down below, in Peterhead, Aberdeen, Glasgow, Edinburgh, Sheffield, Manchester, London . . . fingers stretched towards the knobs of the radios, giving the valves a few seconds to warm up before the six o'clock news.

It was good news.

But the best news of the war was taking place just north of Aberdeen at a height of three hundred feet. A German crew were delivering into the hands of the American and Canadian pilots the weapon with which the Luftwaffe was destroying the British night bomber attacks. Whole. Untouched and free.

At six o'clock the chimes of Big Ben preluded the announcement :

Here is the news, and this is Robert Robinson reading it.

He told how the Axis resistance in Tunisia was now completely disorganized. How twenty-two thousand prisoners had been taken in the previous three days, how the Air Force had continued to batter at the land and sea escape routes and how the King had sent congratulations to General Eisenhower.

32

The Russians, Robinson reported, had reached a new German defence line at Novorossisk, and the head of the Gestapo in Poland had been shot by an execution squad of the Polish underground movement.

A spokesman at the Allied headquarters in Tunisia told the B.B.C.s military correspondent, Major Lewis Hastings, that 'the enemy is in a hell of a mess' in their desert war. As Hastings reported, 'Just as at Alamein, the Axis command was first misled about our dispositions when their front was pierced, and immediately afterwards, the fanning out of the Allied armour dislocated the whole of their defensive positions, and flung them into confusion.

'This dislocation or disintegration can best be realized by thinking what it was like yesterday to be a subordinate German commander, say a battery or battalion commander, somewhere in the hills north or south of the Tebourba road. The first thing that would probably happen is that all cable connections with headquarters would be smashed by the British barrage. Then observation posts would be obliterated or overrun. Ammunition and other things would begin to get short, and there would be no sign of any supplies coming up. British artillery and mortar fire would come from totally unexpected quarters. Then even the wireless link would be put out of action, and the ruin would spread.'

It was a tremendous victory, and the confidence that at last Britain was winning, grew throughout the country. The Scots reached for the bottles of whisky kept in the cupboards to drink a toast in celebration; it was Sunday and the pubs wouldn't be opening that day. But in England, eyes flicked towards the clocks, and many a dog prepared to be taken for a walk. The pubs opened at seven o'clock and the time was five minutes past six.

Flight Lieutenant Roscoe leading Blue flight from Dyce, flying Spitfire BM 515T with Sergeant Scaman behind and to one side of him in AB 921, were flying low and flat out. The Junkers 88 to which they had been inexorably led by their ground radar was in sight.

Schmitt's reaction was instant. All three of the German crew had been scanning the skies, waiting for just this moment. Visibility in the Ju 88 was not good. The windscreen was divided into two sections making it necessary for the pilot to move his head to keep a close look-out. They had no idea which direction the fighters would come from. They were flying south, down the coast from Peterhead towards Aberdeen and it was Schmitt in the left-hand pilot's seat who caught the first glimpse of the Spitfires, coming in from the sea, having already cut off the German plane's escape route.

His hand moved to the selector lever on his left which operated the hydraulic landing gear, and as the undercarriage lowered and added to the drag of the aircraft, it jerked and slowed. Rosenberger on the right side slid open the window of the cockpit and began firing red Verey flares as fast as he could reload the pistol. And to add to the general impression of surrender, Schmitt moved the control column to and fro so that the wings of the plane waggled – the universal sign of surrender.

It was just in time. For Roscoe and Scaman, the Junkers was an easy target. Against the Beaufighter, its British nightfighter counterpart, and even the Mosquito, the Ju 88 with its heavy armament, general manoeuvrability and tight turning circle was a match. Against two Spitfires, in daylight and over the English coast where it had a long, long haul to get back to base even if it were to come out of the combat unscathed, the Junkers stood no chance.

Roscoe knew the surrender signals for what they were, and in the middle of his attack approach, called Scaman over the air and told him to abandon the attack. 'He must have seen your face. He's given in,' the American said in his slow drawl. He waggled the wings of his own plane to let the Germans know he understood the signal, and moved to a position alongside the Junkers so that he could have a good look at the crew. Scaman he told to fly behind and to one side ready to attack from the rear if there was any sign of treachery. In the Junkers, Schmitt and Rosenberger gave deep sighs of relief. The *real* moment of danger had passed. They gave grins of relief to the pilot of the Spitfire on their left, and Schmitt took his hands from the column to wave a greeting. Satisfied, and knowing that he was putting himself in a position of danger, Roscoe passed the Junkers and took up a position in front of it. He kept an eye on the mirror to watch its movements, and those of Scaman bringing up the rear, but enough to one side for him to be seen in Roscoe's mirror.

Roscoe began the wheel that would take all three aircraft towards Dyce.

Schmitt again operated the lever which retracted his undercarriage, but was careful to maintain his exact position even though it meant throttling back the engines as the drag disappeared and the lines of the aircraft asserted themselves. He didn't want his action to be misunderstood. Scaman who had left the safety catch of his guns off, ready to react instantly to any move the German might make, relaxed slightly again when he saw that the Junkers was content to follow his leader into Dyce.

The radio message that Rocoe sent back to base, notifying them of the 'capture' of the Ju 88 electrified the camp. Schmitt had chosen it for its quietness, well away from the dangers of Biggin Hill or Tangmere. But as in all quiet communities, little passed unnoticed. An Aberdeen policeman's young son, whose hobby was aircraft recognition, saw the plane and its Spitfire escort heading for the airfield. He paused long enough to tell his father of the incident before getting out his bicyle, and pedalling off.

Miss Dorothy Smith was having tea with her mother and sister at their home in Dyce, at a window which overlooked the airfield flight path. There was a momentary pause as she refilled the cups, and realized that the plane landing on the strip bore the Swastikas and black crosses of the Luftwaffe.

Another who went for his bicycle was Gordon Forbes, who saw the planes come in over his home in Bankhead, and raced to Dyce for a closer look.

Even as Group Captain J. W. Colquhoun, the Station Commander of R.A.F. Dyce was being summoned to take the surrender of the plane, a large section of the local inhabitants were on their way to the field to see the ceremony.

They were joined by every non-sleeping serviceman and woman on the station, from the Belgian Squadron Commander, Squadron Leader E. G. A. Seghers, known to his pilots, as 'Gin', downwards.

In an atmosphere closely akin to farce, the greatest coup of the British Secret Service was played out, to a wide, appreciative and uninformed audience.

For the equipment that Oberleutnant Schmitt carried on the Junkers was the catalyst which resolved an internal

Bomber Command versus Fighter Command struggle in the R.A.F. and resulted in Air Chief Marshal Sir Arthur Harris, 'Bomber' Harris, pushing through his bomber offensive against Germany, helping to bring Germany to her knees, with the minimum losses for the R.A.F.

Schmitt, Rosenberger and Kantwill handed the secrets of the German nightfigher system to the R.A.F. on a plate, and in doing so, paved the way for the destruction of the Ruhr, and R.A.F. supremacy at night over the skies of Germany.

CHAPTER FIVE

OBERLEUTNANT HEINRICH SCHMITT, aged twenty-nine, was an anti-Nazi. Pro-German, but anti-Hitler. He was also a British spy.

Since the early days of the war, he had been feeding back through his father, and via Switzerland and Portugal, everything he learned about the Luftwaffe, the strength of its bomber force, the state of the morale, and latterly the secrets of the nightfighter defences, particularly those of his group in Denmark – the section over which most bombers were routed on their way to Germanly.

Oberfeldwebel Paul Rosenberger was his friend and accomplice. Partly Jewish, he had yet managed to escape the attentions of the S.S. and the Gestapo, one of the few with Jewish blood to serve in the Luftwaffe, and kept there by the friendship of Schmitt. It was Schmitt who vouched for his loyalty to the Fatherland, and the wounds he had received in fighting for his country helped the pose. But Rosenberger knew that when suspicion finally fell upon Schmitt because of the strange lack of success they had as nightfighters, his stay outside a concentration camp would be brief.

Oberfeldwebel Erich Kantwill, the mechanic, who knew little except the workings of airplanes was still a fanatical follower of Hitler, and despite the gradual wearing down of his confidence by Schmitt and Rosenberger, in his heart he still dreamed of a German victory.

He was the first man into the crowded cockpit of the Junkers, squeezing past the two slightly more comfortable seats of the pilot and wireless operator, taking up his own position on a small canvas seat, over the breeches of the Oerlikon cannon – another of his responsibilities. He was surly. He knew that the other two had scant regard for him, and he felt rather like a non-member of a members only club. The empathy between Schmitt and Rosenberger was great,

they had been flying together for some time, since long before
the air duel over the skies of England when their plane had
been shot-up by British fighters, partly because Schmitt
refused to aim to kill his attackers. The mechanic on that
flight, the third member of Schmitt's original crew, had been
seriously wounded, and even Rosenberger had received flesh
wounds which had kept him out of the air for some time.
Kantwill had replaced that first mechanic – a setback which
Schmitt had not anticipated.

One advantage had been gained however, his skill in nurs-
ing the crippled fighter back to base, on one engine, had been
applauded by his comrades in the squadron, had won him
renewed respect as a flier, and had given him another year
away from suspicion. It would have been easy, the other
crews agreed, for Schmitt to have surrendered himself and
his plane, and allowed everything to fall into the hands of
the British. The fact that he hadn't done so showed his
determination for the cause.

Kantwill strapped himself into his seat. Again he went over
the arguments in his mind. Schmitt and Rosenberger had
assured him that their action in NOT firing at the British
bombers was right. It only resulted in retaliatory fire from
the gunners on the planes, not always effective, their shooting wasn't very accurate, but it *had* resulted in losses. The
empty seats in the officers' and N.C.O.'s messes pointed to
that. Whereas, *they* had survived another year, and if they
were clever, would survive the entire war. And what greater
achievement could there be than that?

Finally, the two constantly pointed out, did he want to
make his new wife a widow, and his young daughter father-
less?

He had talked it over with Anneliese, his wife, when he
went home on leave to Dortmund. What should he do?
Should he report his officer? That was the snag. Schmitt *was*
an officer, whereas he, Kantwill, was merely an N.C.O., a
new member of the crew, whose pilot's flying ability was
legendary on the squadron. Neither Schmitt nor Rosenberger had committed any overt act which could be regarded
as treachery, although their plane's record of success was a
big zero on the squadron scoreboard.

Anneliese's answer had been frightfully logical. 'If they

are traitors, report them and they will be arrested,' she advised. But Kantwill didn't know if they *were* traitors. They had talked to him of *escaping*, and had warned him that they might have to run away. He had even told Anneliese that if he didn't come back from a mission, she wasn't to be too worried when his squadron told her that he was missing. He would return, perhaps after the war. His talk only confused her, probably because the talk of Schmitt and Rosenberger only confused him.

He wasn't sure what to do – exactly the situation intended by Schmitt and Rosenberger. Kantwill was the weak link in their scheme. They hadn't been able to break his loyalty to the Führer, the most they could hope for was to confuse his loyalties – to his country or to his wife and child?

Rosenberger gave him a quick glance as he followed Kantwill into the cockpit, and took the right-hand seat. Kantwill's truculent face told him all he needed to know. He hadn't spoken to anybody, except perhaps to his wife. That was good enough. Even if, and the possibility was most unlikely, Anneliese decided to report her husband's suspicions now, it would be too late. They had brainwashed Kantwill well. If he *had* reported to the Gestapo officer, he would have found an eager listener. There was no love lost between the Geheime Staats-Polizei and the Luftwaffe, and any little rumours which could possibly discredit the fliers were seized eagerly by the black uniformed state police. Of course, there would have been a penalty *had* Kantwill gone to them, not that it would have helped Schmitt and himself much. Kantwill would have been ostracized by every other man in the squadron, and no other aircrew would ever have flown with him again. Living as they did in such small communities, they *had* to trust each other, and no pilot or wireless operator would ever trust a man who might report their slightest indiscretion, slightest criticism of his leaders, to the Gestapo. Schmitt and he had weighed the possibilities carefully in their efforts to subvert Kantwill completely. They had failed to do that, but they had rendered him ineffective, and that was good enough.

Schmitt was the last man in. He seated himself on the left of the aircraft and began the pre-flight checks. A tall, aesthetic, thorough man, he did them carefully, there was

39

going to be no minor malfunction which would abort *this* flight, for he knew in his bones that it was going to be his last one – unless he came back a hero. And he could only achieve that by shooting down the British. He had spun it out well, not another death on his conscience since that awful raid on Guernica, and here it was May 1943, with himself, Rosenberger and of course Kantwill still alive.

It was the Guernica raid, and the arguments of his father, which had converted him from National Socialist to a Social Democrat. From a bomber's height, raining bombs on what he had been told was a war target, the Guernica raid was nothing more than he had been trained for. What he had seen for himself when, with other members of the Condor legion, he was taken on a tour of the razed town, had shown him what bombs on an undefended city could do. He had begun to listen to the arguments of his father, a leading member of the Social Democrat party and at one time, the secretary to the Foreign Minister of the Weimar Republic.

Because of Schmitt senior's lowly role in the Social Democrat Party, and his son's achievements as a pilot, he escaped the dragnet of the Gestapo purges of all enemies of the Nazi régime. He stayed behind in Germany while his friends were either swept up into the concentration camps, or fled the country and set up the German resistance to Hitler in London. There, they co-operated with the British Secret Service in setting up an underground network of spies through Europe and into Germany itself – with Herr Schmitt at the German end. And much of the information that he fed back to Britain came from his own son, fighter ace Oberleutnant Heinrich Schmitt.

Heinrich Schmitt was one of the few members of the Luftwaffe able to take a detached view of life under the Nazi régime. Even in 1940, when the German successes were at their height, with France and the Low Countries overrun, and Britain apparently fighting hopelessly, he had begun to notice the other side of the coin, the bombing and machine-gunning of refugees, and the sudden disappearances of friends, who vanished from their homes in the night, never to be seen again.

One of those to vanish was his own fiancée, a Jewish girl,

who was arrested one night, with thousands of others, and murdered in a concentration camp.

To the Gestapo who arrested her she was just another Jewess, one among millions. But it meant a total turning point for Heinrich Schmitt whose anti-Nazism then became absolute. It set in train the wheel which did more to cripple the German war effort, and bring Germany down, than anything.

He applied to be converted to a fighter pilot, passing his training easily and was commissioned. At least he would never have to bomb anyone again. The British Secret Service was also delighted. If Britain was to take the offensive war into Germany, and send bombers over, the more it knew about the German air defences, the better the chances of success.

They were already building up a picture of those defences, gleaned from information sent back by resistance workers in the countries the Germans occupied, Schmitt's contributions completed a large part of the picture. He was one of their best spies.

CHAPTER SIX

THE British Secret Service had many other successes. Another of their spies was a high ranking officer on the staff of the German General in charge of the Wehrmacht Weapon Office, responsible for development of secret weapons. It was he who gave them the first warning of the development of the V1 and V2 weapons, and set in train the operation by the R.A.F.'s Photographic Reconnaissance Unit which finally tracked down the sites on which they were being prepared – and had them bombed. His information was tied in with that obtained by a young French girl who, in August 1943, seduced a German officer attached to Peenemunde, and obtained from him in their pillow-talk, a detailed account of the beginning of the Flying Bomb organization, the V1 weapon. She confused matters by telling the Secret Service in her reports that the organization was for the V2 rocket, but when her information was added to that of the officer attached to the Weapon Office, the British had a clear picture of the enemy plans.

Professor R. V. Jones had laid down guide lines for the Air Section of the British Intelligence Service. Agents were divided into three categories, those who spied for money; those who liked excitement, and those whose ideals conflicted with the ones of the power on which they spied.

The two best sources were those spying for excitement and idealism. The professional spies were usually inferior, and included too many charlatans, as recruitment depended on personal recommendation which usually came down to 'getting your friends in'.

There was no doubt into which category Schmitt fitted. From him, the R.A.F. learned of every change in the night-fighter procedure in the Danish zone. A star or rocket sent up from the control tower was the signal for the fighter, revving its engines on the runway, to take off.

British fighters began looking for stars and rockets to be sent up, and swooped upon the vulnerable fighter, before it had a chance to gain height, sending it crashing down on to its own airfield.

The take-off system was changed to a green light flashed from the tower. The rockets were abandoned.

There was great need by the British for any information Schmitt could feed through. The Germans' own ground-radar system, Wurzburg and Giant Wurzburg radar sets which picked up the oncoming British bomber streams from forty miles away, and the Lichtenstein radar sets fitted to the nightfighters, making interception in the air comparatively easy, were wreaking havoc with the British bombers. The losses on raids into Germany were frightening the Air Staff. So extensive and successful had the night air defences become, that by 1942, one in twenty bombers sent in raids over Germany failed to return. Most of these, seventy per cent, were shot down by nightfighters, directed to the bomber streams by the Wurzburg and Giant Wurzburg radar from the ground, until within range of their own Lichtenstein sets which led them to the individual bombers.

The Chief of the Air Staff warned the Cabinet that the bombing offensive planned from May 1st, 1943, until December 31st, 1943, would involve thirty-two thousand, five hundred bombers.

If the German nightfighter defences got no better, it would mean the loss of one thousand six hundred and twenty-five bombers and crews.

But, he added, despite the losses, the offensive would continue.

What Britain needed was to know the secrets of the Wurzburg ground radar and the Lichtenstein air radar. So important was the part that these radar units played that they were patrolled twenty-four hours a day by an armed guard, and a three-kilo explosive charge was built into the base of the apparatus, with a spare explosive charge concealed at a point a few yards away, so that it could be blown up rather than allow it to fall into the hands of the British.

It didn't stop the British from getting their hands on a Wurzburg.

British reconnaissance aircraft had found the first

Wurzburg radar station at Bruneval, France, in December 1941. It was a break-through, a golden opportunity for a combined operation to bring back to Britain the secrets of the radar. There was a perfect landing beach nearby, and the area did not appear to be too heavily defended. The three services agreed that a raid *was* possible, and even more important, had a good chance of success.

With a full moon to help the parachutists, the biggest ever airborne force to be used at night at that time left Britain in twelve aircraft on the night of February 27th, 1942, to capture the Wurzburg. The story of the raid has been well told.

Two months after the site had first been spotted, the British scientists had in their possession the heart of a Wurzburg. Colonel B. F. J. Schonland of Ack-Ack Command had set up a concentrated training scheme on the rapid dismantling of radar equipment, using the British radar as a guide. If the full value of the raid was to be gained, as much as possible of the Wurzburg had to be brought back. Army sappers, trained in what to look for, and an R.A.F. Flight Sergeant C. W. H. Cox, a radar expert, were given the task of bringing back the parts of the Wurzburg that mattered. To get them there, and bring them back, a complete infantry company of Commandos were assigned.

They dropped on the snow-covered Cap d'Antifer, and by 0030 a.m. on February 28th, the station sentries had been overcome, the machine gun posts taken and the barbed wire entanglements opened up. The Army sappers dismantled the giant aerial, and Flight Sergeant Cox traced the wires back to the equipment and began taking the Wurzburg to pieces. When the withdrawal order came, to keep the prearranged rendezvous with Navy landing-craft on the nearby beach, the aerial unit, the transmitter-receiver, pulse generator and intermediate frequency amplifier had been dissembled.

Three prisoners, one of them a radar mechanic, were taken back to England with the party.

The stolen equipment, and the interrogation of the prisoner, enabled Professor R. V. Jones to find the counter to the Wurzburg. He found that it used the local electricity supply and because of that had low power compared with the British radar – and as a result, could be more easily jammed.

With the German device actually in their hands, Professor

Jones and his staff had an easier task of learning its secrets. With its range known, and the whereabouts of the rest of the Wurzburg 'guard-dogs', they were able to pick a path across the occupied countries for the British bombers, helped by 'Gee' – the ground-based navigational aid which kept the bombers on their correct course.

All that was needed now was a Lichtenstein set, for the other half of the German defences to be made ineffective. The British Secret Service sent a message out to Schmitt. It was time to bring him back to safety, the Lichtenstein set with him.

He was not too unhappy when the signal came. For night-fighter crews it was a never-ending life of flying and sleeping, with only the prospect of illness or death to look forward to as the end of their tour of operations. They never had a day or night off, even when the weather conditions were too bad for the British bombers to fly. They had to be on 'stand-by', and as the bomber fleets became more experienced, and even bad weather failed to stop them, the 'stand-by' days became more rare.

The air war over Germany was not only a war between bomber-pilot and fighter-pilot, it was a war between scientists; the two best German scientists, Doctor Plendl and Doctor Kuehnhold against the British team. It wasn't only a war of the air, but of the ether, with radio and radar used as the two weapons, each country devizing counters to the latest radar weapons brought into use by the other, which either helped the bombers bomb the German industry, or enabled the German fighters to shoot the bombers down.

But when it came to it, the latest radar aid was only . . . an aid. It could only help the British bombers to beat the German defences. It could only help the German fighters to outwit the British defences, and get to the bombers. Both sets of planes still had to be flown by men. For Schmitt and the other fliers in 10th Squadron, it meant a day that began at dusk, after an intermittent daytime sleep, interrupted only by the activities of the riggers and fitters as they checked their planes and the engines. Important, but noisy. The station commander and the adjutant became no more than a hotel manager and hall-porter to the crews, who seldom saw them.

Each night, Schmitt led his crew into the briefing room where he and the other nightfighter crews were told the state of the weather, and the opinion of the H.Q. on whether a bombing raid was likely or not. If one was expected, the crews were on 'Eagle', the code-name which consigned some crews to sit in the cockpits of their planes, at instant readiness, while the more lucky ones were on fifteen minutes stand-by.

If there was the chance of a quiet night, the code was 'Dove' – thirty minutes stand-by, but in the dispersal rooms, each with its own dining-room, sitting-rooms and bedrooms. There, at least, they could sleep, or rest. There, too, Schmitt, Rosenberger and Kantwill were the one constant factor. Other crews might fail to turn up for the dusk briefing, to be replaced by new, fresh teams, straight out of flying school. But, as Schmitt told the enquirers, his plane had two advantages – it had one of the best pilots in the Luftwaffe, and the plane itself had been charmed.

There had been many unpleasant moments, as pilot after pilot, heading for the number of victories which would earn him the Ritterkreuz, the Knight's Cross, coveted by all Luftwaffe fighter pilots, failed to return. Still Schmitt was there, and still with the zero that stood against his name on the Squadron scoreboard.

Schmitt saw the name, with its number of victories erased from the board, saw another, new name drawn below his own on the scoreboard, both bearing a zero alongside them, and said nothing. If the child was lucky, his name might move above his own as the zero became a figure 1, or 2 or perhaps more. But sooner or later, the eraser would wipe it out to start again with a new name. When particularly likeable members of the mess had been killed, and the other pilots commiserated with each other in Schnapps, he had been challenged about his lack of success, but there had always been a more experienced pilot to draw the aggressive one away, and remind him of Schmitt's war record. But the tension everywhere was growing, as the bomber forces became larger, the weight of bombs dropped heavier, and the entire nation of Germany lay open to attack by the Lancasters, Stirlings and Halifaxes at night, not to mention the Flying Fortresses and Liberators of the daytime. As the pressure grew, the sympathy for Schmitt's bad luck declined. The only solution the Luft-waffe could offer was to throw more and more planes into the air, more and more frequently.

After losing the secrecy of their Wurzburg radar, they con-solidated their night defences with radar screens linking up searchlights, anti-aircraft guns and the nightfighters. Ground radar stations covered Southern Norway, Denmark, Western Germany, Holland, Belgium and Northern France. They reached as far east as Stettin and Berlin, and as far south as the Rhineland. Three thousand radar stations, which, the Luftwaffe boasted, could track the course of a fly if it had the temerity to fly in from Britain. Having tracked it, they could send up a nightfighter with its Lichtenstein radar, home it in, and then when within its own radar range, leave it to shoot the intruder down. It was the pride and joy of the General charged by Goering with keeping the British bomber raids down, General Kammhuber. To the fury of his British counterpart, Air Chief Marshal Harris, the Germans began to gain ascendancy.

The death rate of British planes and crew began to climb. In March 1942, the casualty figure was 4·8 per cent – almost five out of every one hundred planes sent over Germany. In April it was 5·2 per cent. By May it had risen to 6 per cent. Britain was losing the war of the ether, and Harris was insisting that something had to be done.

Not all solutions were scientific. No. 5 Bomber Group had discovered that an empty beer bottle could work wonders with the belt of searchlights and anti-aircraft guns stretch-ing southwards across from the Zuider Zee. The group was convinced that they were radar controlled, and the whole structure hinged upon a master-searchlight, conspicuous by its blue tinge. If this could be doused, the ack-ack fire was reduced and its accuracy impaired. Rear-gunners of No. 5 Group became expert as empty beer-bottle bomb-aimers, dropping them from their rear turrets towards the master-searchlight, when it was switched on. Bomber Command doubted its efficiency, but was content to let the crews loose with their improvised coconut shy. If they *thought* it helped them on their mission, then it *did*.

What Bomber Command wanted was a counter to the new German radar and radio devices. They had found a way to jam the Wurzburg, although it still left the German night-fighters with their Lichtenstein sets able to find the bombers at close range. And in addition, on August 9th, 1942, the Germans found a way to jam 'Gee', the navigational system which had picked a path for the bombers, avoiding the most highly defended areas. The British scientists worked non-stop for eight days to find the answer, and came up with it on August 17th, an anti-jamming device which put 'Gee' back into operation again. The score in the radar war? One all.

For the next year, it was a scientific chess game, with strange moves, bearing strange names as each country attempted to beat the other. The British invented 'Moonshine', yet another radar device, but one which made the reflection of one aircraft on a radar screen look like a dozen. Eight aircraft, fitted with it gave the same signals to the German Wurzburgs as one hundred. Or so the scientists claimed.

To test it out, eight Defiant aircraft of 515 Squadron were fitted with 'Moonshine' on August 6th, 1942, took off from Northolt R.A.F. station, did a few circuits at Portland, and then returned sedately to base. Other R.A.F. planes patrolled the coast of France to watch the German reaction. It was swift. As soon as their radar reported the Defiants, which, or the Wurzburgs looked like a major one hundred bomber raid, the balloon barrage at Cherbourg was raised, and twenty-six nightfighters sent up to intercept the expected attack – the maximum effort the sector could supply.

The scientists and the R.A.F. were delighted, but as a check, sent an exactly similar flight out on August 12th – but this time without 'Moonshine'. The Germans ignored the flight altogether.

'Moonshine' worked, and from then on, small groups of planes were sent out to patrol quiet parts of the British coast while the German radar crews worked themselves to a frazzle tracking bomber forces on a large scale which never seemed to get anywhere.

Worse, the nightfighters were scrambled, night after night and kept patrolling areas without a sight of a British bomber. It did nothing to help Schmitt's score – nor that of any other pilot in the squadron, while it put them on edge, and wore them down with frustration as, despite every effort, straining every last ounce of power from their engines, they still failed to catch up with the elusive bombers, Schmitt was prepared to accept it philosophically. It didn't make any difference to him anyway, he wasn't going to fire his guns at any plane that got in *his* sights.

But these were minor triumphs for the R.A.F. The Luftwaffe was gradually gaining ascendancy in the ether war. Flying, even against 'Moonshine', gave the nightfighter pilots more experience and more confidence. They became more efficient in the use of their Lichtenstein sets, and on the real raids, were knocking down more and more bombers. 'Bomber' Harris needed better countermeasures, and what infuriated him was that he knew that Britain had them, the snag was to drive those in power to use them.

They were thin strips of metallized paper, which were codenamed 'Window'.

'Window' came in different sizes, measured exactly to reflect particular radar wavelengths used by ground and air equipment so that it would fill the radar screens with false blips behind which the planes of Bomber Command would be invisible. To the German radar operator, it would look as if he was being attacked by a whole Armada of aircraft, greater even than the thousand bomber raids.

But the Air Council was worried because it suspected that the Germans also had the device, and if Britain launched it over Germany, the Nazis would retaliate over Britain, and put the British radar system out of action in exactly the same way. Rather than risk this, the Air Council kept procrastinating, waiting for some form of decision which would break the stalemate.

It came on May 9th, 1943, when a Junkers landed at Dyce.

CHAPTER SEVEN

It wasn't the first time that Harris had waited with eager anticipation for the arrival of a German aircraft on one of his airfields. Back in 1941 there had come into his hands the opportunity of ending the war quickly, in one swoop. Somehow, he didn't know how, it had failed. He had taken all the precautions he could, made all the arrangements that had to be made, and that could be made, but that coup had come to nothing – and there were many other high-ranking officers in the R.A.F. who had known about it. They had all been sympathetic, understanding, but Harris felt that some of them had enjoyed his discomfiture. Any other coups he engineered would not get the same preparation as the Hitler plot of February 1941.

It was no less than the abduction of Adolf Hitler by Bauer, his own personal pilot, who would fly him in his four-engined Condor to Lympne airfield in Kent.

Then, the head of Bomber Command was an Air Vice-Marshal at R.A.F. headquarters, and it was there that he established the links with the underground in Germany, with Schmitt and his father. And it was one of those links that brought him the opportunity to bring the war to an early end, even though, at that time, Germany was on its path of triumph. Without Hitler's leadership, and dynamism, few doubted that a peace could be arranged between Britain and the German High Command.

Bauer, Hitler's own 'Flying Chauffeur', much decorated and much respected in Germany for his loyal and devoted service to Hitler, offered Harris the chance of the greatest abduction of all time.

The first overtures were made by his father-in-law, a Bulgarian called Kiroff who called in on the British Attaché in Sofia, in December 1940. The offer the little Bulgarian made was one which startled even the imperturbable British diplomat, who was then sitting on a volcano which was middle-European politics at that time. His inclination as Kiroff told the purpose of his visit was disbelief, but nevertheless, he forwarded the call and its purpose back to Harris in London.

In the cool, panelled office on the piece of British territory in Sofia, with its walls hung with pictures of the King and Queen, and of Winston Churchill, Kiroff explained that his daughter was married to Bauer, and that she knew that he had become disenchanted with Hitler and the Nazi régime. Two of his brothers, also in the Luftwaffe, had been killed, and his own life was a constant round of duty, either actually flying the Führer, or standing by to take him on one of his tours of inspection of the countries he had already occupied, and those he planned to dominate. He was the only pilot Hitler would trust with his life. He held a unique position in the Luftwaffe where his apparent devotion to the Führer was undoubted. He could bring it off.

It was several weeks before Harris realized that it really *was* a feasible proposition. By then, other shadowy men in Bulgaria and in Germany had checked Kiroff's story, had looked into his background and that of Bauer. Everything that Kiroff said fitted. Bauer was of Austrian origin, one factor which endeared him to Hitler, a fellow Austrian. His brothers had been killed on active service against the R.A.F. and he *was* respected and admired by the German population on whom some of Hitler's own prestige had rubbed. Harris put his plans into operation, and devised a scheme to bring Adolf Hitler into the hands of the little R.A.F. station in Kent nearest the coast, Lympne.

On February 6th, at his room in the Air Ministry he outlined to Air Marshal Sholto Douglas, the head of Fighter Command, the fantastic plot that was already afoot, and in a letter on February 21st, told him what plans had been made.

Kiroff, the Bulgarian father-in-law, had gone to Belgrade to get a German visa on a Yugoslav passport he held so that he could visit his son-in-law and daughter in Germany. It was difficult to get a visa in troubled Bulgaria, hence the move to Belgrade. Even this action was treated with suspicion by the British, but the Attaché in Sofia assured Harris that

51

the action was a genuine one, quite feasible under the circumstances that prevailed at that time. And anyway, what had Britain to lose? All that Kiroff carried with him on his mission was an unsigned instruction, with no trace of origin, that Harris had sent out to Sofia in the diplomatic bag. Kiroff had to pass it on to Bauer. It was his flight plan for desertion.

The pilot had not changed his mind. If anything, he was more than ever determined to complete his self-imposed mission. Germany was riding on the crest of a wave of victories, but already there were cracks appearing in the German war machine and Bauer, in his unique position, able to overhear many conversations between his master and his generals, and the conversations between the generals without Hitler's presence, knew that his country was set on a course of destruction. The R.A.F. had not been beaten. Britain had not been invaded. Any nationality other than German were considered second-class citizens and therefore dispensable. And Frau Bauer was Hungarian.

Bauer used his leave to make his own plans, linking them with the written instruction that his father-in-law had smuggled across the border into Germany. Harris had kept it as simple as possible. He had weighed up the possibilities of warning the British fighters, through Sholto Douglas, not to intercept a big four-engined aircraft if it approached the British coast. But there was too much risk of a leakage of information that would be fed back to Canaris and the Abfehr. Bauer and Hitler would have to take their chances against the Spitfires and Hurricanes.

All that Bauer had to do was weave his way towards the Kent coast in whatever fashion he chose, make a steep descent towards the R.A.F. airfield, seven miles from Folkestone and bang the plane down on the ground. If he fired four red flares at thirty second intervals when approached by British fighters, they would not attack. As soon as he landed, he was to stop his engines, put them out of action if possible, and leave the rest to the British.

After their initial scepticism, Harris and Sholto Douglas realized that the whole operation, unbelievable as it had seemed at first, was quite feasible. Hitler in his Condor, and with an escort of Messerschmitt fighters had often flown over enemy territory, usually twice a month and invariably with one or more of his senior staff, while he inspected, from the air, his forces and gave them the benefit of his advice. He had even overflown Britain in that same plane, more as an example of his courage than for any definite purpose.

He seldom flew at night, and Harris didn't expect that Bauer would get the opportunity of edging the big Condor towards the British coast in the hours of darkness. The fighter escort would be suspicious if he tried that. The more probable times would be at dawn, or dusk. He drew up his plan on that assumption, and Bauer agreed with it.

Bauer had one other factor in his favour, his team of co-pilots were all hand-picked – by him, and they were loyal to him. He had alterations to make to Harris' plan, though minor ones. He was always accompanied by at least three fighters which kept at a distance unless signalled. To fire flares if approached by British fighters would inevitably be interpreted as a signal for assistance and would bring the fighters in to his aid. It might only be seconds before the German fighters spotted the British planes themselves, but those seconds could be vitally important in helping him to put the big plane down on the British airfield. He would take the risk of being shot down by the British, and not use the signalling flares. Instead, he had made a number of small yellow metal plaques, bearing his initials, 'A.B.' which he proposed to drop over Lympne as he made his approach. If the British could make the local population aware in some way of warning some official on finding these, so that a last-second instruction could be given to the patrolling fighters not to open fire on the Condor, it was as much help as he could hope for.

Meanwhile, through Sholto Douglas, Harris was making arrangements in Britain to receive his expected guest. Always in his mind was the possibility that the whole operation was a Gestapo engineered one, but though he and Sholto Douglas carried that possibility in mind throughout the entire operation, there seemed no point. At the most, the Condor could beat-up the Lympne aerodrome, launch a gas attack, or produce a secret weapon which would immobilize the airfield for a period, none of which seemed worth a conspiracy of

53

the size they were undertaking. In any event, with a prize like Hitler being offered, the risk was worth taking. He set the wheels in motion.

On February 21st, he asked Sholto Douglas to issue instructions that if a single four-engined aircraft was seen rapidly descending towards Lympne with its undercarriage down, it was not to be attacked or fired at by the ground defences.

There was still the possibility that even though Bauer landed the plane, the remainder of the crew and passengers could overpower him, and take off again. Lympne, at that time, had little in the way of airfield defences, no more than a platoon of young soldiers. It would need a special guard of trained troops, with more than special weapons if the kidnap was not going to fail at the last moment. At that time, Britain had few troops, and even fewer items of special equipment.

Nevertheless, on February 26th, Air Marshal Sholto Douglas instructed the chief of his No. 11 Group, Air Vice-Marshal Trafford Leigh-Mallory to prepare for the arrival of a German deserter at Lympne. Not even Leigh-Mallory was told the real explanation, so close was the secret kept. In a letter, boldly headed, 'Landings by Enemy Aircraft Deserting From the German Forces', Sholto Douglas told him : 'It is not impossible that enemy aircraft crews may attempt to desert. In particular, there is reason to believe that an aircraft of the four-engined Condor type, flown by a German deserter, may attempt to land at Lympne by daylight.

'It is necessary to keep this matter entirely secret, and it is only to be divulged to the Officer Commanding R.A.F. Station, Lympne, who is to make the necessary arrangements on the aerodrome. It will be impossible under the circumtances to issue an effective warning to our fighters, and a deserting aircraft must, therefore, make its way through our patrols as best it can.

'An aircraft arriving with this intent may be expected to approach from seaward in a steep descent towards Lympne with undercarriage down, and if challenged by our fighters or defences, to fire four red flares to avert attack.

'At Lympne itself, it is particularly necessary to guard

against surprise. The aerodrome defences, therefore, must be instructed that a single enemy aircraft of this type, approaching land and possibly firing flares is to be allowed to do so. If there are more than one aircraft, they are to be treated as hostile and engaged.

'The Lympne defences are to be kept constantly ready for such as eventuality. An enemy aircraft landing is to be held covered during its approach and during and after landing. Steps are to be taken immediately to seize the crew, and our defence personnel must again be prepared against surprise and to deal with opposition if necessary.

'An immediate precaution should be to immobilize the aircraft by chocks or other obstacles. Should the aircraft forestall this with an attempt to take off again, it is at once to be disabled or destroyed by A.A. or fighters. Any fighters on the aerodrome at the time should be sent up to patrol overhead, ready to prevent the escape of the one that had landed.'

CHAPTER EIGHT

THE year between the end of 1941 and 1942 showed the turn of the tide of the German fortunes. By the end of 1942, though few people in Britain believed it, and even fewer in Germany, Britain and the Allies were coming to the fullness of their strength. In 1941 they appeared to be at their weakest. Leigh-Mallory's job of providing a force capable of holding Hitler's Condor, Hitler himself and his hand-picked bodyguard was a source of worry. Not only to him, Sholto Douglas and Harris, but to the man who was directly responsible for ensuring the capture of the German leader, and on whom blame would fall if it failed, Squadron Leader D. H. Montgomery, the Commanding Officer of Lympne, and the holder of the lowest rank in the plot.

He was unique in another respect, he had the only revolver on the R.A.F. station.

It did have one hundred rifles, though whether there was ammunition to fit them was doubtful, and it also had seven officers and one hundred and fifty other ranks of the 70th Buffs, on airfield defence, armed with sixteen Browning machine guns, seven Vickers machine guns, two anti-tank rifles, one Bren gun and twelve ·300 Lewis machine guns. Again there was doubt as to whether the ammunition supplied for the weapons fitted, or was indeed fireable. Weapons and ammunition in Britain at that time were in very short supply. There was, indeed, an Armadillo armoured car, again mounted with a heavy machine gun, but its value was more than doubtful, as the armoured car had been unserviceable for some time. However, another Armadillo was sent in to replace it, the machine-gun was remounted on the new vehicle.

For additional reinforcements, Brigadier Hayes, the local Army Commander, although not included on the 'need to know' network, was told that something rather important could happen at Lympne, and realizing that it was more than an anti-invasion exercise, sent a section of three Bren-gun carriers to help the defence of the airfield. He also put a battery of six 25-pounder field guns in a position to bring them within range of the airfield, and attached a liaison officer to Squadron Leader Montgomery so that, if their assistance was required, there would be no delay in bringing it into action.

Four Bofors guns had also arrived, and were divided into two sections, one for anti-aircraft use, the other for ground defence. And another twelve revolvers were issued to the airfield on loan. Lympne was ready to welcome its guests or its invaders.

By March 7th, the plot was thickening well. Harris was able to let the Chief of Fighter Command know that Kiroff had given his instructions to his son-in-law, who had offered his own counter-proposals. Their meeting had taken place in Vienna, the Austrian capital. There was still no question of Bauer having second thoughts, he was as determined then as he was at the beginning of the enterprise. His only other suggestion to the scheme Harris had prepared was that a red beacon should be lit on Lympne aerodrome, and he gave as his target dates the morning on or after March 25th.

His timing caused a minor problem. He gave the zero hours as between five and six in the morning and six to eight in the evening. It was Harris who spotted that he was thinking in terms of Central European Time, whereas Britain still had its clocks put back, to conserve the hours of daylight. The new dates and timings were passed on by Sholto Douglas to Air Vice-Marshal Leigh-Mallory on March 10th – fifteen days before the crucial day. Bauer carried on his duties, flying the leader of Germany on his flights, and waited for the opportunity to arise when he could put the plane down at a British airfield, and opt out of the rest of the war.

It wasn't easy. Hitler had a soft spot for his fellow Austrian. There were few people he could trust, and he tended to rely upon those who had no opinions about war strategy, whose roles were inferior enough not to make them instant war-pundits, and who were prepared to accept him as he was. That wasn't easy either. Hitler wasn't a particularly attractive human being. Those who accepted him as he was, he treated well. Bauer was one of those who enjoyed the Führer's favour. It sickened him just as much as it had sickened the man who had kept the war diary at the Führerhauptquartier, until he was transferred because he was thought politically unreliable. It could happen at any time to anyone. And Bauer knew it could happen to him. He could be transferred at any time to an active service unit, flying bombers over Britain, or earmarked for the Russian offensive where his chances were, he knew, odds against.

Bauer didn't know it, but Britain already had knowledge of Hitler's personal habits from that same man who had kept the Hitler war diary at his headquarters, and who had been transferred. Harris knew about the Führer's day, which began at 11 a.m. or 11.30 a.m. just before the first reports and briefings were given to him at the Führerhauptquartier. At 2 p.m. he would sleep – like his great rival Churchill – for an hour, before returning to the operations room to receive further reports, and discuss future plans with his chiefs of staff, usually with Jodl and Keitel officiating.

At 8 p.m. with a few of his trusted cronies, Hitler went for supper – another simple meal. The rest of the table could have what they liked, but Hitler had no more than a vegetable stew, with stewed fruit as a dessert, no more than one or two glasses of beer, all of which he ate and drank rapidly, mechanically. For him, it was merely fuel to keep running the fires of his imagination, a means of subsistence. Although he had finished his repast in a few minutes, the meal itself lasted two or three hours, as he encouraged his generals and guests to talk. *Their* glasses were constantly refilled. *His* remained empty.

One snag for the smoking members of the entourage was that he forbade smoking in his presence, it was thought because of his susceptibility to laryngitis. There was another one. Hitler quite often disengaged himself during the meal, turning his thoughts inwards, and ignoring the conversations that sprang up around him. But for the unfortunate few who didn't know, he was quite well aware of the drift of conversation, and would suddenly join in, not with a conversation piece, but with a monologue about something he had either read or learned, and which had stirred him.

From then on, he would control the conversation for one

or two hours at a time, holding forth on the subject, and defying contradiction from anyone at the table. And, because of the gift he had of simplifying the most complex problems, he was a difficult man to argue with. Most of his guests preferred not to.

As a dinner companion, Hitler left much to be desired. He bit his finger-nails, he would run his index finger backwards and forwards under his nose, for him the dining-room held little difference from the bathroom.

Supper ended usually at 10 p.m. when the Führer and his staff officers would receive the latest records in the operations room, and hold a final conference until midnight or 1 a.m. Then with his more trusted confidante, he returned to his private quarters for a final snack, a record session – usually Wagner or Beethoven – and a special cake baked for him. It was this cake which caused his stomach upset and his beer belly, a source of worry to him in the later stages of the war.

But as Bauer well knew, Hitler was a man of moods, and a man unable to sleep well at night. Even at 2 a.m. he was still wide awake, taking a walk in the open, preferring the early to the later hours of daylight, it was thought because he was afraid of the sun and its effects upon his brain. Not until 4 a.m. would he retire to his bed, for a two hour reading session, before inducing sleep with some drug, and then begin his day at 11 a.m. the following morning. It was from the books he read then that he formed the opinions that he expounded to his commanders later that same day. The last read, the most emphatically told – a fact that the leaders of his armies knew well.

The fact that Bauer knew his master's moods so well made him aware of the fickleness of the position he himself held. It needed no more than an instant to relegate him to the ranks of aircrew, destined for the most dangerous missions, anywhere. There were enough examples, ones he knew quite well.

There was that of the Oberst, who received a telegram from Rommel confirming an earlier communication which had been sent to Hitler of his intention to withdraw from a position in the North African campaign. In view of the previous telegram, Hitler's staff officer decided that it need not be brought to the Führer's attention. It was the wrong decision. When Hitler saw it the following morning he called the duty officer before him.

'If you say as much as one word in your own defence I shall have you shot,' he fumed. The officer had no idea what wrong he had committed, but as Hitler ranted on, it became clear that he should have brought the second telegram to him as soon as it appeared. After having more and more abuse piled upon him, the Oberst left Hitler's office, as a private in the Army. That same day, with a heavy pack upon his back, as a common soldier, he was made to make an hour's march to the railway station for service as a member of a unit on the coast of France.

There was another case years later which would have given Bauer room for thought. Oberst Meichsner, commander of the Organization Section of the Wehrmachtuhrrungsstab, OKH, was a trusted friend of Hitler. He was one of the officers approached during the bomb plot against him on July 20th, 1944, but because of the trust that Hitler had placed in him Meichsner refused to participate in the conspiracy. During the trials of the other plotters, his name was mentioned as having been approached. The refusal to join it didn't save him. Hitler ordered that he be hanged with all the rest, because he had not revealed the attempt.

Small wonder that the Führer made no friends. The only one Bauer knew of was Rudolf Hess. Hitler loved him as he would a brother, perhaps because he felt that there was a latent insanity in him, an affliction which often caused one brother to love the afflicted one more. He was solicitous over Hess' welfare, and refused to allow him to make inspection tours of the front, except for one occasion when he made sure that the deputy-leader never came within range of any firing. To make sure, Hitler personally warned the officer of the General Staff escorting him that there would be severe punishment for him if anything happened to Hess. Even after his disastrous flight to Scotland, he bore the loss of his only confidant stoically, never giving any outward sign of the hurt he had suffered.

Bauer wondered if the British would reunite the two once again when he completed his mission.

The problem for Harris and Sholto Douglas was still secrecy and security. The Air Ministry was worried whether the security arrangements were adequate, and sent the Director of Ground Defences, Air Commodore A. P. M. Sanders to inspect them. Were they sufficient to pin down the Condor once it had landed? He thought not, and told Sholto Douglas so. Another two Armadillo armoured vehicles were sent in, and the drome was put on an R.A.F. station basis, which meant more troops to help in guarding it.

There was still left the problem of what to do with the prisoners once they had been captured. Air Vice-Marshal Harris offered his suggestions on March 18th.

'I feel that it will be essential to get the prize (or prizes if there are more than one of great price) away from the scene of the "accident" at the earliest possible moment, in case of any immediate attempt at interference by an escort or by hastily summoned air support. I consider therefore, that the booty should be brought straight up to the Air Ministry by car under armed escort, and would be glad if you will give orders to that effect. Sanders has arranged for a V8 box-body touring car with driver, and two motor cycles and riders to be sent down to the Station for this particular purpose, all of which will arrive there today.

'If there is a large bag, only the biggest birds need be sent in the Ford, the number being limited to a maximum of two so as to allow for an adequate close escort. Any others could be dealt with later.

'As it would be most undesirable to extend the circle of those already in the know, I do not propose to lay on any special arrangements at this end unless and until we hear that something is in the net. It will be essential therefore that a telephone message should be got through at the highest priority either to me, to Sanders or to Boyle, if anything occurs at the coast. Will you arrange this too?'

Sholto Douglas could and did. The instruction to send whatever Lympne 'bagged' was forwarded to Leigh-Mallory the following day. The chief of Fighter Command added his own precaution however, he ordered that a spare car and motor-cycle escort join the Ford V8 when it brought its passengers back to the Air Ministry. Just in case.

The eventual conclusion was pure farce. While Lympne itself and the rest of Kent went about its normal business throughout March, as the first available date for the

61

defection came closer, the tension mounted. The secret was well kept, but it would have taken the dumbest of fools to have been unaware that something was up on March 25th. It wasn't often that the Commanding Officer, and every other officer was up and about at 7 a.m., scanning the sky in a seawards direction, tensing at the sound of every engine. It wasn't normal for every gun to be manned with the best available crew, for every fighter on the station to be warmed up ready, and for every pilot to be in a state of readiness.

And it wasn't normal for the hot-line between the Station and the Air Ministry in London to be in constant use as Harris and Sholto Douglas waited to hear if the birds were in the net.

Harris in his letters had been emphatic about the dangers of Bauer landing, and then another pilot taking the aircraft up again while the ground defences gaped in surprise. It had happened before when a German aircraft landed by mistake on a British airfield and had been tamely allowed to take off and escape. But it wasn't going to happen while Squadron Leader Montgomery was in charge of the station. The R.A.F. men on the station were armed, and were supported by the Young Soldiers of the Buffs and two platoons of the 2/6th Queen's Regiment. The crucial hours after dawn passed on the 25th, and so did the dusk hours on the same day.

Every day from then on, the Station stood ready. By April 9th, anti-climax had crept in. The evenings were drawing out, the German successes were mounting and there was boredom at Lympne. Squadron Leader Montgomery was having difficulty keeping alive enthusiasm on his station – and at the Air Ministry. Worried, he asked for another Bofors gun to improve his defences. But Air Commodore Sanders refused to add any more to the four already on the station. He pointed out, on April 11th, that there were other urgent uses for the guns – including 'one in connection with the Battle of the Atlantic'.

By May 17th, Sholto Douglas and Harris realized that Bauer's bid had failed, but they kept the preparations going for another two weeks. The Condor didn't come, although by then there were other frequent visitors from Germany to R.A.F. Lympne, all engaged on strafing raids.

The chapter ended on May 28th when the Air Ministry

ended the 'Special Arrangements – Lympne' as from June 1st, ordered that the Ford V8 six-seater be returned to the No. 4 Motor Transport company from which it had been borrowed along with the motor-cycle escort, and the troops were returned to their unit.

But the experience wasn't entirely wasted. The lessons learned were borne in mind by Harris when a more successful defection came to be arranged.

CHAPTER NINE

BUT while Air Chief Marshal Harris waited for his Air
Council to come to a decision about using 'Window', the
losses of his bombers were rising. More and more were being
left behind in the raids on Germany, with their irreplace-
able crews. He warned the Air Council on August 26th,
1942, that if a sustained and effective bombing operation was
to be carried out, there had to be countermeasures to the
German defences.

It wasn't the first time that an attempt had been made to
get radio countermeasures on the high priority list. Air Chief
Marshal Peirse, who had led Bomber Command in 1941 had
tried to. Air Chief Marshal Sir Sholto Douglas (now) had
said that the countermeasures needed accelerating in March
1942. But the letter from Harris revealed the figures of his
bomber losses. The conclusions he drew were inescapable. If
nothing was done, Bomber Command would be whittled
away to nothing by the German nightfighters. Bombers were
being shot down quicker than the factories could build them,
and the flying schools train the pilots and crews. To lend
emphasis, the Director-General of Signals added that despite
'Gee', it was no longer possible to find a route through to
Germany which didn't require the bombers to pass over
heavily defended areas. Everywhere was now defended. The
Germans had completed the defensive wall to protect their
home country.

The Air Ministry could no longer close its ears to the pleas
of Harris. On October 29th, 1942, it gave Bomber Command
full authority to take the war into the ether as well as the air.
Radio countermeasures were put on the high priority list.
And the jargon of the R.A.F. began to include even stranger
words than previously.

Germany's radar screen had been developed to the extent
that, from their advanced radar stations, they could actually

'watch' some British airfields, and see the bombers take off. All they had to do was follow them on their path towards the Continent, and at the latest possible moment, send the night-fighters up to intercept. The range of these Giant Wurzburg radar sets was one hundred and twenty-five miles, and it was intolerable to Harris that so many of the movements of his bomber force should be under such close observation. The answer provided by the British scientists was 'Ground Mandrel'.

Three enormous structures were built in the Dover and Hastings area which pushed the German radar cover back one hundred and twenty-five miles to twenty-five miles. Similar, but smaller 'Mandrel' sets were fitted to eighty of the bombers taking part in the raids, and to Defiant aircraft of No. 515 Squadron.

The 'Mandrel' bombers, interspersed among the attacking forces would provide cover from the radar while they were in the air, and the Defiants, patrolling the enemy coastline twenty miles from the shore between Don Helder and Cherbourg, would keep the German radar screen pushed back. The Luftwaffe no longer had all the time in the world before getting ready to take on the bomber waves, and they were no longer able to overlook the British airfields.

Then came 'Shiver'. As early as October 1940, pilots of Bomber Command reported that strange things happened to the German defences when they switched on their I.F.F. sets (Identification of Friend or Foe). The sets sent out a signal which identified itself as friendly to other British aircraft, but some pilots noticed that when they switched the sets on, as many as thirty searchlights which had been comb-the skies were suddenly switched off. Even searchlights as far as ten miles ahead of them would suddenly be doused.

The scientists concluded that the searchlights were radar controlled, and that the return signal from the I.F.F. sets upset the radar readings. Engineers modified the I.F.F. sets on all British operational aircraft, fitting a switch, the 'J' switch, so that interference could be produced automatically and continuously.

With 'Mandrel' and 'Shiver' a start had been made in reducing the German superiority in the ether war. 'Mandrel' was first used in December 1942 in the raids on Mannheim,

Duisberg and Munich, and on each occasion, the night-fighters which had been expecting their usual long advance warning, were taken by surprise.

It took only a few months for them to discover however, the way that the British were jamming their radar screen, and by February the Defiants patrolling the German coast were being attacked themselves.

By June 1943, the Operational Research Unit of Bomber Command provided the disturbing news that the losses of the bombers carrying the 'Mandrel' equipment had shown a significant increase. Germany had discovered a counter to the 'Mandrel' counter.

The British Secret Service reported that the 'Mandrel' sets from two crashed bombers had been salvaged and given to the Telefunken company. Telefunken had devized a hom-ing equipment which was being fitted to the nightfighters. Known as 'Freya-Halbe' it had a range of seventy miles, could pick up the beam of the 'Mandrel' set as it was used against the German ground radar, and follow that beam straight to the bomber carrying it. As a result, while the total bomber losses on one raid were 5 per cent – a high enough figure – those of the Halifaxes fitted with 'Mandrel' were 21 per cent.

It would have been the end of the 'Mandrel' jammer, except that Fighter Command had the solution already. They had been concerned with exactly the opposite situation in December 1942, German aircraft with jammers that inter-fered with the British ground radar.

They also had developed a homing equipment, similar to the German 'Freya-Halbe'. But in trials, they had found that if the jammer was used intermittently, the problems of hom-ing in on it were greatly increased.

Switch the jammer on for a minute, and then off for a minute, and it was possible to jam the radar without giving time for the British nightfighter with its homing equipment to find the attacker.

Reverse the situation, and the counter to the 'Freya-Halbe' homer was ready.

By the middle of June 1943, the 'Mandrel' sets were fitted with an attachment which switched themselves on and off automatically, and prevented the fighters homing on them.

By the following month, the Germans had extended the frequency range of their ground radar, so that the 'Mandrel' jammers couldn't reach the frequency. The scientists at Telefunken had learned other things from the equipment they salvaged from the crashed bombers, they had learned the limitations of 'Mandrel'. It would have taken months to fit all the bombers with modified 'Mandrel' sets capable of jamming the new frequencies, so in July 1943, 'Mandrel' was abandoned. It didn't matter too much, for by then the tests on the Lichtenstein set were well on the way, and the best anti-radar device of all was about to be employed.

There was another target for the British scientists apart from radar – radio itself. If the R/T link between the Ground Control Interception station, and the nightfighters they were controlling could be broken, the information gained by the Wurzburg sets on the ground as to the actual whereabouts of the British bombers could not be passed on to the fighters in the air. They would be forced to rely on their own limited range Lichtenstein equipment and 'freelance forays'.

It was another piece of British luck that just the right way of achieving this was already in their possession. A British wireless operator in a Handley Page Hampden of No. 5 Group was flying over a defended zone of Holland in September 1941, when on tuning his radio to the German wavelengths he found a lot of R/T coming through at 3,665kcs. He felt in a mischievous mood, tuned his own transmitter into that frequency, and screwed his Morse key down. Five minutes later he listened in again, and found the enemy station was *still* trying to pass the same message. He reported the incident, and talked of the fun he had had at the expense of the poor German radio operator on the ground. A bit of amusement, there was nothing like messing up the Jerry defences – but it was remembered when Bomber Command wanted nothing better than to break the radio link between the ground and the air.

It was the germ of the idea that became 'Tinsel'.

There were strong arguments against its use. No-one on either side wanted to start a 'jamming war' which would render the air-waves useless for any form of communication for either British or German planes. Another argument against using it was that the German H.F. radio bands were

67

the same as the British ones, and would interfere with the British Direction Finding and Regional Control facilities. And, those against pointed out, the Germans would switch to the V.H.F. bands.

But as the Luftwaffe was already beginning to jam British communications in the Middle East from the ground and the air, the go-ahead was given.

A small portion of the German frequency band was allocated to each bomber, and the wireless operators in each aircraft listened in on their particular section until they heard the German R/T operators. Then they tuned their own sets in, and transmitted a jamming note – the sound of the engines of their own aircraft picked up by a microphone.

The bombers began using 'Tinsel' in the beginning of December 1942, and by the end of the month it had proved a complete success. Germany had to develop a new communication system, the Fuge 10, covering another V.H.F. band – but this had already been anticipated, and a new transmitter, covering just those bands, was coming off the British assembly lines. They were fitted into the bombers and 'Tinsel' continued. The Germans could no longer direct their fighters by radio once they were in the air.

CHAPTER TEN

As the muted peals of 1942 rang out, and the glasses were raised to toast 1943, and the end of the war, there was no doubt who was winning the war of the air – Germany. The Airborne radar was in considerable use, and was causing a a great deal of worry to those in charge of the ever-growing bomber offensive, not least to the crews who saw, with increasing fatalism, the mission success average drop and drop. The life of a bomber crew was short. The newer and fresher the crew, the shorter the life. The Tour of Operations stretched further and further into the distance.

The Lichtenstein radar was winning the war for the Luftwaffe.

British scientists were not idle. They had the counter to the Lichtenstein in 'Window', but there was argument within the R.A.F. as to whether it should be used. In the meantime, they did their best with ground jamming equipment. 'Grocer', a station set up at Dunwich on the East coast, was specially designed to counter the Lichtenstein. Its development wasn't easy, and it was complicated by the fact that the Lichtenstein was beamed, and its direction depended upon the course the aircraft was flying. If the German nightfighters were flying towards the jamming installation, results were much better, but the Germans weren't always so obliging.

'Grocer' couldn't provide the antidote that the bombers needed for the Lichtenstein equipped nightfighters, and the pressure to use 'Window' grew.

Just as British radar was instrumental in bringing down the greater number of German bombers attacking Britain in the Blitz, the situation was reversed once the Germans lost the initiative in the air. As 'Bomber' Harris constantly reiterated, in his arguments to introduce 'Window' over Germany, not only would it reduce the number of casualties to his bomber forces, it would improve their bombing accuracy if they weren't disturbed by the defences, and it was obvious that the more experienced they became, the greater was their efficiency – if they weren't shot down. In addition there was a side-benefit, ground crews were encouraged if they felt that the planes they were servicing were going to return, and not be left crashed in Germany.

From January 1942 until July 1943, when the arrival of Schmitt and his Lichtenstein equipped Ju 88 resolved the matter, the arguments for and against the use of 'Window' had swayed backwards and forwards.

In May 1942 the Chief of the Air Staff, Air Chief Marshal Sir Charles Portal, sent to Prime Minister Winston Churchill a memo summarizing the arguments for and against its use, and came down heavily in favour of using it, for Bomber Command.

But he pointed out the snags. While the few experiments they had carried out, over the sea, when the wind conditions were such that the strips of metallized paper would fall nowhere near land, showed that it interfered considerably with the enemy radar and searchlight equipment – it also interfered just as successfully with British radar. It would make the interception of German bombers by British fighters much more difficult.

However, he wrote in his memo, the subject had been examined by the Radio Policy sub-committee of the Chief of Staff's committee, and they recommended that its use should be sanctioned.

The Admiralty, he said, had no objection. The War Office thought that the strips would interfere with its own defensive radar, but had no objection to 'Window' being used by Bomber Command, if the Air Staff were satisfied that Britain would thereby gain an appreciable advantage over enemy defences.

Leader of the anti-'Window' camp was the Commander-in-Chief Fighter Command, Air Chief Marshal Sir Sholto Douglas, who felt that if Britain used 'Window' on its bombing raids, it would introduce the idea to the Germans, who would employ the same tactic to great effect against the British ground radar and the radar-equipped nightfighters.

Churchill's principal scientific adviser Lord Cherwell agreed with him.

That same month, a memo was sent to the Vice-Chief of the Air Staff which did nothing to help the arguments for the use of the weapon which contributed more than anything to beat down the German defences.

The Secretary of State was involved, and on July 17th, he sent a memo to the Chief of the Air Staff, Sir Charles Portal, saying that he had heard that the tests of 'Window' carried out by Fighter Command had alarmed the Fighter Command Chief. Could he see the report?

It was sent to him that same day. The Chief of the Air Staff gave it as his opinion that the report was decisive against using 'Window' at that time, but he added that it raised the question of whether training should be started in case the Germans used it.

The Secretary of State endorsed the decision not to use 'Window'.

What had turned the scale was the unequivocal opposition from Air Chief Marshal Sir Sholto Douglas, who on July 15th, 1942 spoke to the Under-Secretary of State at the Air Ministry of the Fighter Command tests.

His most experienced Observers had proved, he said, that no amount of practise would enable his fighters to overcome the effects of the device if it were adopted by enemy bombers. The responses from the metallized strips was far too strong and obliterated the responses from the aircraft.

He considered that the results of the trials proved that the possible use by the Germans of 'Window' was a most serious menace to the British night defence system, and that there were no means at the moment of reducing or overcoming that effect.

If they did, the vast amount of work which had been put into the production of the various scientific devices which had enabled night interception to be brought to a reasonable degree of efficiency during the past two or three years would be completely wasted. As no alternative devices exist, the position would become extremely serious were the enemy to discover the effect of the leaflets.

He asked that any proposal to use 'Window' against the

enemy radar be abandoned, and that any personnel who had anything to do with it be warned that the greatest secrecy was to be observed with regard to the results obtained.

As far as Air Chief Marshal Sir Sholto Douglas was concerned, 'Window' worked. But too well.

Exactly the same controversy, for the very same reasons, was raging at exactly the same time – in Germany.

On July 19th, 1942, at Berchtesgaden, Hitler called a conference of his top associates to discuss the use of their equivalent of 'Window'. They called it 'Fenster'.

Attending the meeting were Field-Marshal Goering, Herr Doktor Spanner, Admiral Raeder, General Field-Marshal Sperrle (the man who led the Condor Legion in Spain during Schmitt's early flying days) Field-Marshal Von Beck, General Rommel and two scientists.

Goering explained that a new method of interfering with the British radar system had been perfected. It would upset the British techniques, which had become so effective that the Luftwaffe had been forced to abandon deep penetration bombing, and concentrate upon attacks on shipping and coastal targets. Goering proposed that Sperrle should be allowed to use 'Fenster' on deep penetration targets, and over heavily defended areas.

Fortunately for the British night defence system, exactly the same arguments against using the weapon were put forward. One of the scientists pointed out that while Britain had a bomber force that was increasing, the Axis air resources were already at their maximum.

And though the Allies were achieving considerable penetration into Germany by night at a strength 'which was having very serious moral and material effect on the country, statistics showed that the Axis method of controlling guns and searchlights by radio methods had been most effective and were taking increasing toll of the British bombers'.

If 'Fenster' were used now against the English, they would easily be able to copy it, and would then be in a position to counter the best Axis defence.

And as a clincher he added that the metallized material would interfere with their own ground defences, particularly as radio was needed for the direction of Axis searchlights in the defended belts of Holland, Belgium and North West Germany.

The other scientist, who had disagreed with his colleague throughout the meeting added quietly, but with a smile at his colleague's discomfiture, that 'dark' hunting by scientific methods (with the Lichtenstein) had proved so successful that the searchlights had now been removed from the night defence belt in the West.

Field-Marshal Von Beck pointed out that a decision on this important matter must depend on the results of military operations on the Russian front during the summer. If these were successful, he said, then a major part of the Luftwaffe would be released for operations in the West, and, in particular, an increased number of fighters would be available for protection against British raids. If, on the other hand, Germany was unable to knock out Russia that summer, or worse still, if the Russians counter-attacked successfully, continuing their efforts through the winter, then it would be a very different situation. Berlin might well come within air striking range of both the British and the Russians under circumstances in which both countries could bring a very heavy scale of attack to bear. In these circumstances, it would be necessary for the German defences to be operating at the maximum degree of efficiency.

While 'Fenster' might help the Axis air offensive against Great Britain it would have no effect against the Russians whose system of night defence was not very scientific. On the other hand, the moment 'Fenster' was used over Great Britain, the British would inform their Russian allies who would then be in a position to use this very simple device over Berlin to protect their night bombers from the highly developed anti-aircraft defence over the capital.

Von Beck concluded that for these reasons, 'Fenster' should not be used unless the Russians were knocked out of the war.

Discussion continued in the same vein until the Führer, having announced that his patience was exhausted, ruled that the Luftwaffe should not, for the moment, use 'Fenster' but should continue developing it. In particular, methods of countering this weapon should be developed by the Luftwaffe in the event of the British using it. He urged Doktor Spanner to push ahead as rapidly as possible with the perfection of his infra-red airborne equipment and explore the possibility of using this technique from the ground. It was possible that the British had already thought of 'Fenster' and might use it at any moment against Germany. This emphasized the importance of pushing ahead with counter measures. If and when the British used 'Fenster' against the Axis, General Field-Marshal Sperrle would be free to employ the weapon against the British.

Great minds thought alike.

In Britain, as the bomber losses continued to mount, the attitude against using 'Window' was softening. On April 2nd, 1943, in the Air Council room at Whitehall, the Chief of the Air Staff called a meeting of top Air Ministry officials, the heads of Bomber and Fighter commands as well as the supply services and Lord Cherwell of the Cabinet Offices. It was to discuss solely whether ' Window' should be employed.

The question was : 'Is it agreed that the use of "Window" would be likely to be of substantial assistance to our bombing offensive?'

There was no doubt in the mind of Air Marshal Harris. He told the meeting that, from the point of view of losses sustained during the past winter, they had been lucky. Weather had helped to keep the German nightfighters down, and there had been assistance from 'Tinsel' and 'Mandrel'. Nevertheless, failing additional aids, he anticipated an inevitable increase in losses. The arrival of 'Monica' (another radar device, fitted in the tail of the aircraft to warn of the approach of nightfighters – not too successful) should help, but it had been long delayed and would not be ready until the end of April. Even then, it could only be used on the Halifax bomber. He thought that 'Window' should be used as soon as possible, and that it would be of great assistance to Bomber Command – assuming that it was as effective as was estimated.

One of the scientists attached to Bomber Command added that on the calculations which had been supplied, 'Window' would save one out of three aircraft lost at present by enemy action.

Doubts came from the Air Ministry, and one of their representatives, the S.A.T. said that in his view, the claim that 'Window' could save half the British losses due to radio-controlled or A.I. fighters, and half those due to radio-controlled ground defences was not based on any firm evidence. He felt that on previous experience of new devices, the claim was too high. This was discussed at some length and it was felt that in the paper which was being prepared for the consideration of the Chiefs of Staff, it should be pointed out that the claim should not be regarded as factual, but as a reasonable estimate.

The meeting came to a compromise conclusion on the question before them. They agreed that 'Window' would be likely to be of substantial assistance to the bombing offensive *provided that it were suitable for employment against Aircraft Interception radar as well as Ground Control Interception, and was used as a complement to existing methods and devices.*

Having come to a decision on that question, the meeting had to come to one on the follow-up. 'Is it agreed that in strategy and tactics there is now a strong balance of argument in favour of increasing the effectiveness of our bomber offensive by the use of "Window"?'

This posed the problem, whether there was sufficient retaliation if Germany used 'Window' over Britain.

Fighter Command thought there wasn't.

They said that if 'Window' were used efficiently against this country, the efficiency of the U.K. night fighter defence would drop by as much as eighty to eighty-five per cent and this was a serious consideration which had to be set against the estimated saving of bomber aircraft by our use of 'Window' over Germany.

The Chief of the Air Staff leaned towards the use of the device. What had to be taken into consideration, he said, was that the Germans were in no state at the moment to maintain any serious offensive against Britain. It was estimated that they would maintain fifteen to twenty sorties a day against us at the moment, rising to perhaps thirty during the summer. By cutting this down they might be able to launch a maximum force of one hundred and fifty bombers in one night, including the use of aircraft and crews from training units.

In his view, the present strategic position would justify Britain in using 'Window' as soon as possible, but it was clearly a matter which would have to be considered by the Chiefs of Staff and subsequently by the War Cabinet.

Once again, the conclusion backed both horses. The meeting agreed that the use of 'Window' in the near future would be recommended from a strategical and tactical point of view, *but that the probable effect on the efficiency of our night defences if 'Window' were used against us should be clearly appreciated.*

However, the crunch question put to them at the end of the meeting brooked no argument.

'Is it agreed that the use of "Window" be authorized as from the middle of April 1943?'

It wasn't quite agreed. Instead, they agreed that a recommendation should be put forward to the Chiefs of Staff that 'Window' should be employed as from May 1st, 1943.

The Chiefs of Staff met later that month, they had before them a note by the Chief of the Air Staff outlining the history of 'Window'.

Sir Charles Portal recalled that when they met on April 27th, 1942, they had approved the proposal to employ the device as a countermeasure against the enemy radar, but since subsequent experiments showed that the effect of 'Window' on their own A.I. was likely to prove serious, he had decided that it should be withheld until (a) their own Radio Direction Finding equipment could defeat it or (b) they were confident that a large scale bombing offensive against Britain would no longer be practicable for the Germans in the light of their war with Russia.

Now, however, the Air Staff considered that on balance it would be advantageous to introduce this countermeasure at an early date. In view of the far-reaching implications of such a step, he now asked the Chiefs of Staff to confirm the decision they gave in April 1942 and to approve the use of 'Window' on operations as from May 1st, 1943.

He gave as his arguments that the German Radio Direction Finding systems consisted broadly of four types of equipment:

(1) 'Freya', an early warning system which could also be used for fighter interception.

(2) Large 'Wurzburg' which had a narrow beam and

was mainly used for the control of fighter interception.

(3) Small 'Wurzburg' for the control of unseen fire from the ground.

(4) 'Lichtenstein' equipment for the completion of an interception when the aircraft was controlled by a large 'Wurzburg' or for free-lance interception when there were large concentrations of bombers.

Against 'Freya' the British were using ground and airborne 'Mandrel' jammers, and trials in Britain indicated that 'Window' could make the remainder of the enemy radar devices largely ineffective.

He added that although it was difficult to assess the actual effect which would be obtained in practice against the enemy radar, it was considered that the efficiency of the enemy equipment would be halved by the use of 'Window', and he added that this was regarded by experts as a reasonable assessment.

Spelling out the chilling figures of bomber losses over Germany, the Chief of the Air Staff told his colleagues from the other services that the Germans were greatly expanding their nightfighter defences, which were already regarded as being responsible for 70 per cent of the bomber losses by enemy action.

In 1942, 5·06 per cent of bombers sent against Germany were destroyed. He emphasized what that figure meant by spelling it out in numbers.

Of the twenty-two thousand, three hundred and forty-five bombing sorties despatched against Germany at night in 1942, one thousand, one hundred and twenty-nine were missing or destroyed by enemy action.

If 'Window' had been employed, it had been calculated that three hundred and sixteen bombers would have been saved – and the seven men who crewed each plane.

Emphasizing the importance of choosing May 1st to launch the anti-radar device, he told the Chiefs of Staff that from that date until the end of December 1943 Bomber Command would send at least thirty-two thousand, five hundred bombers against Germany, as Air Marshal Harris launched his one thousand bomber raids. That figure represented 70 per cent of Britain's bombing effort.

Using the 1942 figures for comparison, Britain would expect to lose one thousand, six hundred and twenty-five aircraft and their crews.

But if 'Window' were employed, it would save four hundred and fifty-five of them.

While the Chiefs of Staff endorsed May 1st as the date for launching 'Window', there were still doubts in the minds of many. Despite the worries of Sir Sholto Douglas that retaliation by the Germans with a 'Window' material would incapacitate his fighters, the argument of 'Bomber' Harris that the Germans hadn't got the bombers to take advantage of it was the convincing one. However, the launching date was delayed again. May 1st came and went. 'Window' was not employed. Bombers were still being shot down unnecessarily, said the seething Harris.

At just the right moment Heinrich Schmitt delivered into the hands of the British what everybody wanted to know, and evaluate. The efficiency of the German Lichtenstein radar.

On May 27th, 1943, Air Commodore S. O. Bufton, the Director of Bomber Operations sent a letter to Air Marshal Harris.

'Sir, I am directed to inform you that the provisional date for the start of "Window" operations is the 1st July, 1943. I am to request that you will make all the preparations which are necessary for the launching of "Window" on that date.

Existing security measures are to be maintained and no "Window" material is to be dropped until the executive instructions are given.

I am, Sir,
Your Obedient Servant.'

The first 'Window' raid was against Hamburg on July 24th/25th.

CHAPTER ELEVEN

ROSCOE and Scaman kept their two Spitfires in tight circles as the Junkers came in to land at Dyce, ready to pounce if it showed any inclination not to obey the implied threat of their machine guns. They need not have worried. Schmitt had no intention of doing anything but put the big plane down on an airfield in Britain. He concentrated on making a good landing – his last one.

The Junkers needed flying. Fast and manoeuvrable as it was, with a performance better than a Beaufighter, and in many ways, the Mosquito also, its history as a dive-bomber showed in the layout of the controls. They were close together in the cramped cockpit, and care had to be taken when they were used, it was easy to mistake one for another. He put down thirty degrees of flap, and as his speed dropped to two hundred and fifty kilometres per hour, lowered the under-carriage. It slowed the plane noticeably. Down came the rest of his flaps, and as the aircraft became tail-heavy because of the automatic trimming of the elevators, he re-trimmed it. He wasn't going to have any criticism from the R.A.F. pilots about the flying abilities of the Luftwaffe It was a flap approach, and he used all the landing-strip to slow the plane down after he touched. He could have banged the brakes on, but there was going to be nothing undignified about *this* landing, and he was going to take no chance of the plane slewing. The R.A.F. would want to test this aircraft, and he was going to give it to them in perfect condition.

On the airfield, there was a scurry of confusion. The guard was turned out, although the guard commander was un-certain what to do with his small picquet. The arrival of Group Captain Colquhoun solved the dilemma – he ordered them to 'Present Arms', and waited for further instructions from the Station Commander.

'Stand the men at ease', said the Group Captain, 'and be

ready to guard that plane when it lands. No-one must go near it.' The guard commander was happier, he had his orders.

Flight Lieutenant W. J. H. Childs, the commander of the R.A.F. Regiment unit recently attached to the airfield brought up his unit to reinforce the guard, and formed them into a line ready to march out and surround the aircraft when it taxied to a stop. He wondered whether anyone had thought to issue ammunition to the men. The canteen and N.A.A.F.I. emptied in a rush, while the less curious glued their noses to the billet windows. Nothing like it had ever happened before at Dyce, or anywhere else.

Within minutes, the perimeter fence was lined with spectators, who had arrived on their bicycles to see what was going on. Group Captain Colquhoun slapped down as firm a security as he could, but there had been a breakdown in communications somewhere, and he hadn't been notified that the Junkers was expected.

Hardly had the plane's wheels touched down than the locals, R.A.F. and civilians, were reaching for their pens and writing paper, to pass on the news of the biggest local excitement to hit Aberdeenshire since the war started. Those who weren't writing were on the telephone, and though a special mail and telephone intercept was set up, it was too late to stop everything that went out of Dyce.

What *were* checked were two thousand, five hundred and seventy-eight letters, of which more than four hundred contained either eye-witness or second-hand versions of the defection. Air Ministry and British Intelligence were horrified. Britain had been at war for four years, and still the public and even servicemen and women hadn't registered that the eternal poster, 'Careless Talk Costs Lives' was more than valid.

Of those four hundred plus letters, twenty-four were confiscated altogether, and never reached their destination. Nine of them were sent by R.A.F. men, the remaining fifteen by W.A.A.F. girls.

But, as was pointed out to the Air Ministry, an event like the capture of a German aircraft, or even the shooting down of one, was a matter of rejoicing – unless there were special circumstances about it. As far as Dyce and the rest of Aberdeenshire were concerned, this was a matter for congratulation. So, the pens went down on paper and the telephones were picked up.

Two telephone calls which were intercepted resulted in an exchange of memos between Group Captain Colquhoun and the Headquarters of No. 17 Group. One was from a caller at Allied Airways at Wick, who provided the civilian air-route between Britain and the neutral countries, to his opposite number at Dyce airfield.

Wick : 'Hello, Ian?'

Dyce : 'He has just left at 16.21.'

Wick : 'He will be here at 5.20 then.'

Dyce : 'It's "A.H." today. Paton, he had a lovely take-off, first time he had flown it.

'A Junkers 88 was taken into Dyce yesterday by two Spitfires. They gave him a burst of machine-gun fire. They got him in whole, not a mark on him. He is now lying beside the big hangar, looks lovely.'

Wick : 'Is there a dip-stick in the plane for us?'

Dyce : 'I will look it up.'

The Air Marshal commanding Coastal Command administered a reproof to the headquarters of No. 17 group when he sent on transcripts of the telephone intercepts.

'Enclosed herewith are copies of telephone intercepts which indicate the manner in which people are talking about the recent incident at R.A.F. Station Dyce.

'It is thought that the one from Allied Airways is the worst, and it is suggested that someone on the spot might be able to administer a reproof to them for discussing in this manner Service affairs which should be no concern of theirs.'

But as Group Captain Colquhoun found when he in turn was the recipient of the buck, while Allied Airways maintained an incoming and outgoing telephone log, there was no entry recording the call, and any one of six people might have received it and given away the information of the Junkers. He suggested it was a matter for the Provost Marshal and the civil police.

Among the letters which were held by the Air Ministry was one which 'Ethel' of the Motor Transport section sent to Mrs. H. Halloway, of King's Lynn. She wrote : 'A Jerry plane landed the other night, surrendered, and I had the job

81

of driving the prisoners to the guardroom, but they were all dressed up in evening dress under their flying kit. Funny business that he landed with all his load and now we are waiting for something to happen.'

Just the sort of impression which the R.A.F. didn't want to get around.

'Helen' of the station's Met Office wrote to Mr. and Mrs. E. Lowe, of Hove, Sussex : 'I shouldn't be telling you this, so keep your thumb on it or I'll get shot – we were aroused by Florence yelling through the door "Air raid warning red" . . . we looked out, Maisie said, "Oh, it's only a Mosquito" when off went the Ack-Ack . . . shepherded by the new fighter flight, the thing came in and landed . . . and out stepped three Jerries complete – and I think this is pukka gen – with despatch case.'

Leading-aircraftwoman K. H. Paterson, also at the Met office, wrote to Lieutenant Dorkill of Edinburgh twice, but he never got the information either. Both were held by the censors.

In the first letter was the vital paragraph, 'Well, now for some real news. We at Dyce R.A.F. have just been in action and brought in a Jerry. The siren and red went at Dyce tonight, and our Ops Flight took off – they got hold of him over the sea and forced him to land in perfect tack on our drome . . . The three Germans got out and saluted Groupy, then the Spits landed – Fancy pet, a German Ju 88 absolutely intact on our airfield. I'm wondering what will come over the radio about it.'

Nothing did.

The second letter, two days later, would have given the Lieutenant more news about the plane, had he received it. '. . . more about the German plane episode when I see you. I think that it is pretty certain that it was a planned escape on the Germans' part, because the Spits did not give a shot and there was nothing wrong with its engine.'

'Isabel' wrote to Mrs. A. Murray of Northumberland : 'The siren went in camp and we were told that one enemy aircraft was approaching the camp . . . when to our surprise we saw the two fighters coming back escorting another plane which was dropping flares . . . Then he was directly above us, it was then we saw the black crosses on it . . . Then another surprise, he put his wheels down to land. Imagine, land on our drome! Then a voice came over the loudspeakers warning the Ack-Ack batteries not to fire on the plane coming in ... Anyway we, the three of us got right up to the kite and three live Jerries got out grinning all over their faces ... The excitement was terriffic. But after all, it isn't every day a Ju 88 lands on the drome, is it?'

'Elsie' of the M.T. section was another eye-witness. She would have told Mrs. J. Monks of St. Boswells, Scotland: 'We had a great thrill on Sunday, our Spitfires captured a Jerry plane and it was brought in, at least forced to land, so we gained one plane and took the crew of three, prisoners. I watched the whole thing ... of course, keep this to yourself, we are not supposed to tell.'

'Teeny' wrote to Mrs. Murray of Perth: 'We were just sitting in the office when we got the red warning ... about five minutes later we could hear a couple of Spitfires buzzing around and I went out to investigate. I saw a big plane coming in with its undercarriage down, and I said to a corporal who was there, "Look there's a Jerry coming in" ... Just then a message came over the Tannoy for the Ack-Ack gunners to cease firing at the enemy plane which was landing ... When we got down the plane had landed and three Germans were getting out of the plane. Seemingly one of the Spitties had damaged its engine ... and the crew have been taken prisoner and we got a beautiful new Ju 88 on our station now with not much wrong with it.'

Aircraftwoman K. Foster of the signals section was actually writing to her boyfriend Leading Seaman William Poster, at sea with the Navy, when the plane landed.

'Why on earth did I mention raids just now, the siren has just gone ... Some Spitfires have just taken off, must be a Jerry somewhere ... must leave you for a minute can hear gunfire don't want to miss anything. Can see three Spits and they are circling over a big black bomber. My God, it's a Jerry and he has his undercarriage down. Just a sec — Boy oh Boy. Bill they forced him down and he's landed on the drome.'

The achievement in capturing an enemy plane was shared by everybody in the camp. Aircraftwoman Kevan, of the W.A.A.F. section felt some pride in sharing minor victory, and showed it in the letter she wrote to Driver Risby of the Royal Army Service Corps in Scarborough.

'Last night we (Please note *we*) captured(!) a lovely Ju 88 intact with the three German crew. There seems to be something peculiar about it – they came over about 5.30 – our spitties got up after them – there were a few bursts of machine gun fire – then our Ack-Ack guns got the order through the Tannoy not to fire on the enemy as they were coming in to land ... They came sailing in with the white flag flying – two of them calmly combed their hair before climbing out and saluting our Groupy ... The Jerrys are still here living on the fat of the land.'

The censors, however, did not take kindly to her sharing the sense of achievement, and it was another letter that never reached its destination.

It wasn't only women however who were guilty of putting what the Air Ministry considered as classified information down on paper.

'Harry' gave away the details in a letter sent to Mrs. O. Hatton of Manchester. 'The Gerry that landed is one of the latest machines so they say. So there has been bags of panic, lot of big noises buzzing about taking photos of it ... They say that they intercepted it about fifty miles from the coast and they did not fire a shot. I wonder if there is anything funny going on? It does seem strange.'

Aircraftman H. R. Lister of B. Flight was even more loquacious than the average W.A.A.F. In a letter to his parents, Mr. and Mrs. G. Lister of Liverpool he gave details of R.A.F. procedure which in itself would have activated the censor's razor blade – apart from the details about the Junkers.

'We had bags of excitement at about 6.30 p.m. on Sunday. There are five chaps on of a night, and two of our kites had just come on to readiness, that is oxygen turned on, starter batteries plugged in and everything ready for an immediate take-off. The two pilots and the five ground crew rushed out and we had the kites airborne in two and a half minutes ... anyway about ten minutes later we got word that they had spotted a Ju 88 which was firing red flares all over the place as a signal to surrender to our Spits ... There were three Huns in the Junkers, two officers, one displaying the Iron

84

Cross and a Sergeant . . . Don't spread the news of the Ju 88 because it has not been in the news yet.'

The Listers didn't get the chance to tell their friends about the success of their son's squadron. It was another letter which didn't arrive.

There was more than a touch of imagination in the letter which Leading Aircraftman W. S. Bolton wrote to Mrs. J. Hoggas of Kirkcaldy, Fife.

'A Jerry came over our dummy drome which is a mile or two from our camp. He dropped flares which is a signal when a plane is going to land. But two of our Spitfires made him land on our drome. They got one of his engines out of gear so he had to land. There were three men in it Mary, it is a Ju 88, one of them is in our hospital but he is only slightly hurt. You won't hear about it on the wireless for a few days yet . . . The Corporal S.P. who took them to the guardroom says the Pilot Officer is a Norwegian . . . I will let you know the next letter I send you Mary. I think it is an affair like the Hess do myself, or again they may all be Norwegians, Mary, who have got a Jerry plane and escaped from Germany, as they may be fed up with Hitler and his crowd eh? They saluted our C.O., never gave the Nazi salute. They had no bombs in their plane so it looks funny to me.'

Corporal Emmott employed some sarcasm in his letter to his parents, Mr. and Mrs. E. Emmott of Crosshills, near Keighley.

'Well, gen for a change, the news on Monday said: "No enemy aircraft crossed our coast last night!" If that was true, then Dyce aerodrome must have had the D.T.s. I could have sworn that an hour before we finished work on Sunday an aircraft dived over our workshop (a tin Nissen hut) and machine guns *do* sound like what we heard when *we* dived (on the floor), we had sent up two Spitfires to meet an un-welcome visitor and within ten minutes of us going to earth we were dashing across the drome to be "in at the kill". After only *three* bullets entering his engine cowlings the visitor *hung out a white rag* and landed his kite in *perfect condition* on the drome, the latest type Ju 88 and an officer and two airmen came out and gave themselves up . . . Still it might have been a dream. We must believe what the news says, you know, so don't say a word or I'll be up for spreading rumours.'

The Hess surrender, again in Scotland, was in the mind of many of the Dyce personnel. Leading Aircraftman J. Turner of B Flight was another who subscribed to the theory that the Junkers' arrival had similar overtones. In a letter to Mr. and Mrs. Fenwirk of Glasgow he wrote :

'Last night was quite exciting, there has been no mention of it on the wireless or in the papers. But at six o'clock the sirens went, two of our Spitfires took off after Jerry. He was coming in from the sea, they intercepted Jerry about twenty miles out, it was one single Ju 88. It was obvious as soon as Jerry spotted our planes he knew his number was up. So he sent up flares and put his wheels down, this is a sign of surrender ... The crew, one German officer wearing the Iron Cross and two N.C.O.s thanked our pilots for not shooting them down. This seems very strange to me, it might be another Hess business ... But armed guards were there and put them into a car and drove them to the guardroom. Apart from the value of the Ju 88 we shall find out a lot of secrets about it, also I understand the crew were talking freely and giving us a lot of information.'

They were, and so would L.A.C. Turner – if his letter had arrived.

But virtually any letter mentioning mysterious happenings at Dyce was doomed to receive the attentions of the censor, even the rather innocuous one from the Squadron chaplain, Reverend Arthur A. Hamilton, who wrote to his fellow cleric Reverend Squadron Leader Wilcock at R.A.F. Yatesbury.

'One of the most exciting things in the war happened here last Sunday but unfortunately I cannot tell you about it for security reasons and our letters are liable to censorship. However the man who is succeeding Wing Commander Kidd is connected with us here and is reporting for duty at Yatesbury in a week or two so you can ask him about the excitement at Dyce that day. It was a real thrill.'

The Reverend Wilcock was never able to ask. Even the Chaplain's letter was held.

Dyce R.A.F. station was also a civilian aerodrome. Even in wartime the civil air-routes between Britain and neutral Sweden were kept open by B.O.A.C., but without the comfort of airliners. Fast, unarmed, unarmoured planes, the ubiquitous Mosquito was the most popular, ran a regular service between the airfield in the North-east of Scotland and Bromma airport in the Swedish capital, ferrying mail, secret documents, spies and V.I.P.s backwards and forwards across the North Sea.

It led to some curious situations. On one occasion in August 1942, as a Mosquito carrying mail for the British Embassy landed, coming from one direction, a Ju 52 was making an approach from another. The pilot of the Mosquito watched with interest as Joseph Goebbels and his staff from Hitler's Ministry of Propaganda disembarked from the Junkers and stalked to the waiting Mercedes, away from the two planes which were parked side by side.

CHAPTER TWELVE

THE Air Ministry was furious that the news of the landing at Dyce had become public knowledge to a large part of Aberdeenshire. The Station signals officer, Squadron Leader Robert Dawson, was away from camp on the day of the landing, and was visiting Leuchars.

'The first news I had about it was the following day. I was visiting my brother James in Fyvie on my way back to camp, and he told me all about the landing,' said Squadron Leader Dawson, now of Fraserburgh. 'They all knew about it. He thought then that it was a mysterious business, and it certainly seemed like it when I got back to camp. By then it had been repainted in R.A.F. colours, and shortly afterwards it was flown to R.A.F. Farnborough by a Polish pilot with a Beaufighter escort. They had to get special clearance so that it could pass through the radar screen.'

Group Captain Colquhoun had no idea of the furore that lay ahead as he waited on the tarmac to take the surrender of the aircraft and its crew. The heavy rain, mixed with sleet and snow which had been falling all day had gone. So had the cloud-ridden sky, 10/10 at eight hundred feet as the Station's log recorded. It was a fine evening. Group Captain Colquhoun, his adjutant, the officer in charge of the R.A.F. Regiment's anti-aircraft guns and four of his men, all armed, plus two of the Squadron's own station policemen made a guard of honour for the German crew as Oberleutnant Schmitt led them down the hatch of the plane.

They formed themselves in a line before the aircraft, and then Schmitt stepped forward, saluted with the Luftwaffe's own salute, and formally announced his wish to surrender himself, his aircraft and his crew.

Colquhoun wanted them away from the aircraft as quickly as possible, in case they changed their minds and did it some damage, and also in case they had left a destruction device aboard it. He accepted the keys of the plane from Schmitt, and gave them to Flight Lieutenant Childs, R.A.F. Regiment officer, with instructions to see that the hatch into the aircraft was locked. He knew the desire for souvenirs among the airmen and women on his station.

'If anything is taken from that plane you'll answer for it,' he growled harshly before handing the keys to the young officer.

The problem was what to do with the three Germans, for the camp had only two separate cells in its guard room. Colquhoun had the N.C.O.s put in them, while he took the officer to an empty ward in the sick quarters. And it was there, in his broken English, that Schmitt explained the importance of his mission, and that his aircraft contained special equipment of great importance to the R.A.F.

He need not have bothered, for the Group Captain's command of the situation was not to last for long. R.A.F. experts were already on their way to Dyce, with full knowledge of what the plane contained. An Air Commodore from Group headquarters and an interrogation officer landed only one hundred minutes after the Junkers.

The crowd outside the camp grew to stare at the easily identifiable aircraft on the unit's tarmac. The two guards left on duty beside the plane began to fidget as their friends in the Service pressed closer to inspect the first tangible example of the enemy they had seen. One minute's lack of attention or distraction, and the souvenir hunters would be at work. The threat made by the Group Captain to their commander had been passed on to them. If anything went missing they would be for it.

Group Captain Colquhoun too began to feel uncomfortable about the attractions which the plane was offering not only to his station and the civilians, but to any German reconnaissance aircraft, tracing the route of the allegedly ditched Junkers. He had the Air Ministry signalled, asking permission for the plane to be moved into a blister hangar, out of sight. The permission didn't come until the following day however, and a reinforced guard spent an uncomfortable night ensuring that nothing on the aircraft was liberated by the station staff.

In the meantime, Schmitt, Rosenberger and Kantwill

began to talk to the British interrogation officers. They had plenty to say and they said it willingly. The R.A.F.'s knowledge of the German air defences on the Continent, and the British Cabinet's appreciation of the effects of bombing on the German morale took a great leap forward.

Based on what the three men told him, Wing Commander S. D. Felkin produced a report which described in detail the organization, equipment and method of control of nightfighters in the Denmark area, and which could be taken as representative of the German Air Force nightfighter system as a whole. For the first time, 'Bomber' Harris knew exactly what he was up against.

His opposite number, General Sperrle had broken up his nightfighter organization into 'Gabiets' – boxes, each a circular area of some one hundred and twenty kilometres in diameter with a 'Stube' – a Wurzburg radar equipped control site – at the centre. The nightfighter boxes were arranged in groups which were controlled by a headquarters normally sited on the airfield which housed the nightfighters covering the area. The headquarters, known as the 'Fuhrungs-Gefechtssand des Raumstabes', which was normally abbreviated to 'Raumstab', in turn was commanded by a Divisional Headquarters, which in Denmark where Schmitt and his squadron were stationed, was Jagddivisionen 2. This, in turn, came under the direction of the supreme nightfighter command, Fliegerkorps X11, with headquarters at Zeisst, near Arnheim.

Harris learned that the seventeen nightfighter boxes in Denmark were controlled by Raumstab 100, whose headquarters were at Grove. And he even learned that the man controlling the Raumstab was a German fighter ace of the First World War – Oberstleutnant von der Pongartz. Harris and the Secret Intelligence Service were able to make a personal assessment of their foe.

There was much more that Schmitt was able to tell, now that his messages didn't have to be limited to easily conveyed, cryptic facts. He was able to give the code-words used for telephone and teleprinter messages. The headquarters of the German nightfighters, the Fliegerkorps X11 was always referred to as 'Falke 1'. Their divisional headquarters, Jagddivisionen 2 had the code-word 'Nordstern 1', while their own Raumstab was given the Grecian name 'Gyges'.

With these code-words explained it became easier for those monitoring the German order to plan the counter-moves.

The Lichtenstein equipment he had delivered was already being investigated by Professor R. V. Jones, then attached to the R.A.F.'s Scientific division. But Schmitt was able to describe, in great detail, the operation of its matching equipment – the 'Freya' radar which took up the search for hostile aircraft from a distance, and then passed it on to the 'Wurzburg' sets, two of them codenamed 'Red' and 'Blue' which plotted the hostile aircraft and the nightfighter respectively.

Schmitt described the control hut which contained the plotting table covering the operations over the Box, on which the data supplied by the two 'Wurzburg' sets were translated into visual forms. There, on a podium stretching round the plotting table, the Jagerleit Offizier watched as two spots of light, one red and one green – the green one representing the nightfighter, the red one the British bomber – moved, their paths followed by the two 'Wurzburgs'. With a telephone and earphones which kept him in touch with the whole system of control, including the nightfighters over his area, the Jagerleit Offizier, gave instructions to the nightfighter which brought the green spot closer to that of the red one. He had much on his mind. He had to take into account cloud conditions, and even the strength of the wind as he issued the orders which made the nightfighter above move his control column. If he did his task well, the red and green spots on the plotting table began to merge. At that point, the range between the two aircraft, one bomber, one fighter, was no more than two hundred metres – and by that time, the Lichtenstein on board the fighter would be doing its own tracking. At that point, the fighter pilot was on his own. He should already have seen the exhausts of the victim bomber.

But, important news for the British bombers, was that until January 1943 none of the nightfighters in Jagddivisionen 2 had been equipped with Lichtenstein, and at that point, only a few had it aboard. Three Lichtenstein-equipped aircraft recently delivered to Aarlborg were withdrawn within three days to Gilze-Rijen as it was thought that there was more need for them there than in Denmark.

That *was* important news for Bomber Command. It meant that Denmark was a better route to Germany, a safer one for the bombers, than Holland. The planes could easily be transferred back once the bombers were found to be taking the Danish route, but a safer route for only one night meant British lives saved.

Installing the Lichtenstein on an aircraft was not an easy task, as Schmitt explained. First the aircraft was sent to Stendal airfield for the installation of the Lichtenstein transmitter and receiver and the aerials. That took three weeks. Then it was flown to Berlin where Telefunken A.G. fitted the presentation unit and calibrated it. That process took another fourteen days.

There was only one place where the Lichtenstein could be calibrated, at Berlin/Diepensee. The equipment was so sensitive that any variation of more than one millimetre in the length of its connecting cables would affect calibration. So if the equipment on board any aircraft in service were moved, or damaged, the whole aircraft would have to be flown back to Diepensee for recalibration.

Diepensee became an immediate target on 'Bomber' Harris' list.

There was much more information that Schmitt and his crew were able to impart. The standard colour for German nightfighters was black, but it was being changed to a bright blue undersurface with a mixture of brown, green and blue on top, as black was too easily seen, particularly against light cloud. The German nightfighter ace Major Streib flew an aircraft with almost white upper surfaces, and because of his success as a fighter pilot, there would be many who would follow his example.

The warning to beware of light-coloured aircraft was swiftly imparted to air-gunners in the R.A.F. Lancasters and Halifaxes.

A weakness of the German fighters was the radio-telephone system linking them with their ground control. It required too much power to operate this and the plane's own intercom, so the radio operator had to switch off the intercom when he talked to the ground, and then pass on to the pilot the instructions he had received. The frequencies and call-signs used by the German radio-operators were valid for twenty-four hours and were changed each evening according to a chart made out in advance for each calendar month.

Schmitt had thoughtfully brought his chart with him.

He brought some unwitting amusement for the British interrogators too. There had been many complaints from the German radio operators about jamming on the main frequencies used by the fighter pilots on certain occasions. There had even been a lot of bad language – in Swedish.

It was encouraging for the British to know that though Sweden was neutral, there were certain radio operators there prepared to risk heavy punishment for the sake of the British bombers, by making the lives of the Germans that much more difficult.

The supply of information from Schmitt seemed endless. He had gone to enormous lengths during his time at Aarlborg, making notes, drawing sketches of what he knew the British would require. They wanted to know what the operational procedure of a nightfighter squadron was. Schmitt supplied it.

Each morning, the aircraft was checked, fuelled and re-armed. The nightfighter Gruppe was given a Met report for the area it covered, and if it was favourable for Bomber Command attacks, each unit had to supply, by dusk, to the Raumstab, the number of aircraft and crew it could send into the air.

On some bases, two aircraft were sometimes sent up during the afternoon into a Box to carry out vectoring and interception practice on their Lichtenstein sets. These practises were known as 'Zieldarstellung' and the radio-telephone frequencies of the previous night were used. They were training exercises for air and ground personnel.

The R.A.F. didn't need to know much more. A number of Mosquito and Spitfire pilots added to their 'kills' during afternoon patrols of the nightfighter dromes. The Germans abandoned the afternoon training sessions.

In some districts, Schmitt continued, where the R.A.F. were expected every night, there were standing patrols from dusk onwards, and if no raid developed the aircraft carried out practice flights in liaison with ground control.

The information came in useful later on when Mosquitos with a rear-facing radar began 'trailing their coats', and posed as bombers to attract the attention of the Lichtenstein-equipped fighters.

But there was no standing patrol in Denmark, other than the one over the 'Schakay' Box, for the special purpose of intercepting the Courier aircraft which flew between Sweden and Britain.

The patrol which Schmitt himself had been making when his aircraft disappeared.

There were other code-words which Schmitt supplied which helped the British bomber force. The code-word 'Marie' was used to indicate to the nightfighter that it was immediately behind its target. 'Marie 3' meant that it was three kilometres behind its target bomber. Then, as soon as Lichtenstein contact had been made, the fighter's wireless operator signalled back to his base 'Emil Emil' which meant that he had made contact on his set. The code-word for indicating that he could actually see the bomber was 'Ich beruhre'.

The attention of the British bomber wireless operators tuned in to the German wavelengths became more pronounced, and their evasive action on hearing 'Emil Emil' more definite.

Because of the poor downward visibility of the German nightfighters, their attacks were usually made from below and behind, where the bombers were not usually so well defended. The nightfighter schools taught the pupils to aim at the underpart of the bombers between the engines and the wing roots where the petrol tanks were situated. One method of attack was for the pilot to aim ahead of the bomber and fire as he pulled up, so that the bomber flew into the night-fighter's fire which was sprayed along the length of the fusel-age. The Me 110 pilots preferred to pull up perpendicularly and turn to port or starboard while delivering a burst which raked the bomber's wings from tip to tip.

As soon as he scored a victory, the fighter pilot announced it over his radio telephone by the code-word 'Sieg Heil'.

As counters to the attentions of his former comrades, Oberleutnant Schmitt had many suggestions to make to his interrogators. Because the German radar linking ground to air could not cope with more than one bomber and one fighter at a time, bombers should be sent over a Box at the same time. One would be given attention, the others would get through. He added, that the practice should be adopted night after night which would have the effect of wearing out the ground staff and the nightfighter crews, who weren't too plentiful in Denmark anyway.

For an alternative, single aircraft could be sent at intervals into the range of the early warning system, which would result in nightfighters being sent up right away, to patrol their boxes. The effect of this also would be to exhaust the fighter crews who would have to maintain a continuous patrol.

The British improved on this suggestion. They sent Mosquitos instead of bombers. Not only were the fighters exhausted, they were shot down.

Schmitt criticized the tactics of the bombers returning from raids on Germany. They flew too straight for too long, he said, and enabled the German radar to get an accurate fix. He suggested that they should make frequent changes of course and height, a change of course of forty to fifty degrees, with a minimum of thirty degrees. Doing so would make them less vulnerable to the 'Wurzburg' radar, and thus the Lichtenstein fighters.

But the normal tactics of reducing height steadily until the Dutch coast was reached at three hundred feet was viewed favourably by Schmitt. It let them pass through the nightfighter control areas with the greatest possible speed, and made attacks from below almost impossible.

As another criticism, he suggested that the exhaust system of the British bombers should be improved, particularly on the Halifax. They were seen too easily. In fact, Schmitt added, most British aircraft suffered from this fault. One of the Courier aircraft on the service from Britain to Sweden was only shot down because the German fighter pilot, who hadn't been able to get within radar range, saw the flames from its exhaust.

CHAPTER THIRTEEN

THE five men who met over a cup of tea in the A.B.C. café, on a side street in the West End of London, early in the spring of 1943 could have come from anywhere. Thirty years later, the only glances they would have received, would have been for the shapelessness of their clothes, if that. But in 1943 they received far more than a few critical glances, for they were all wearing civvies, ill-fitting, but civilian clothes nevertheless – at a time when the country was very much at war, and anyone of vaguely military age not in uniform was likely to be given a white feather.

These five, however, were more at war than most. One was a Special Intelligence Service Officer, keeping a fatherly eye upon his three charges, three men who only a few days previously had been wearing the uniform of the Luftwaffe, one of them with an Iron Cross 1st class to testify to his bravery. He was tall, slim, elegant and aloof : Oberleutnant Heinrich Schmitt. The second was Oberfeldwebel Paul Rosenberger, small, dark, lively and half-Jewish; the third was Oberfeldwebel Erich Kantwill, taciturn, sullen and very much lost in a strange country.

Making up the party, and buying the tea was one of the R.A.F.'s best pilot's, the second-in-command of the Fighter Interception Unit based at Ford, Squadron Leader Christopher Hartley, who had just taken over the seat Schmitt had vacated, as pilot of Junkers 88 D5-EV, one of the twelve Lichtenstein radar-equipped nightfighters with which the Luftwaffe was gaining supremacy over the British bombers.

The Junkers, now wearing British camouflage and R.A.F. roundels, had been given to the Fighter Interception Unit to test. The R.A.F. wanted to know what its potentialities were, not only against the bombers which it had been designed to attack, but against the nightfighters with which it duelled, the Beaufighters and Mosquitos.

'It was a strange experience. All so unreal,' the former R.A.F. pilot recalled. 'Sitting at a table with three men that I could well have been trying to knock out of the sky only a few days earlier. But I'd been given the job of testing the Junkers, and there were various things about it I wanted to know.

'The only person who could tell me was the German pilot, so it was fixed for me to meet them. It was decided that it would be best for us to talk on some sort of neutral ground. They weren't really prisoners, more like guests. So there we were, sitting around the table in this little restaurant, just as we might have been a few years earlier, discussing aeroplanes. I'd had to borrow a sports jacket and trousers, so as not to be too conspicuous, and to avoid giving any hint as to what I was doing there.

'I'd been familiarizing myself with another Junkers 88 that the R.A.F. had, so as not to risk any damage to the night-fighter, and I'd flown this one in the daytime and at night, to find out what it could do, but there were things about it that only the pilot of the plane could tell me. So I finished up meeting the entire crew, over tea, in a London restaurant, on a spring afternoon, during the war.

'Schmitt didn't speak a great deal of English, but we knew what we wanted to convey. I was worried by a malfunction in the stand-by turn and bank indicator. It wasn't working, and when you're flying a strange aircraft at night, which even the R.A.F. fitters know nothing about, you need to know what instruments work, and if not, why not. I told Schmitt about this fault, and he just nodded and told me to fit a new battery. I fitted one that evening, and the instrument worked perfectly from then on.'

Because it was a 'need to know' situation, and Hartley needed to know nothing about the reasons for the arrival of the Germans in Britain, he asked them no questions about their presence in London.

'We talked mainly about the Junkers, because that was the plane I was mostly interested in, but we talked about air tactics too, and about the other German aircraft. Sometimes Schmitt would check a detail with one of the other two in German, but whereas Rosenberger was quite forthcoming, the mechanic, Kantwill, was a nasty piece of work. Schmitt

97

was obviously a politically minded man, aware of the future. Rosenberger was half-Jewish and looked it, and they were the brains of the trio.

'They'd obviously planned their defection well. They did all the right things at the right time, lowering their under-carriage and waggling their wings, while one of them was firing Verey lights. They knew what they were doing.'

The original intention of the Air Ministry, when the plane was delivered into their hands, was to let the scientists take its equipment to pieces to discover its secrets, said the then Squadron Leader. 'It could well have happened had it not been for Wing Commander Derek Jackson.'

Wing Commander Jackson, D.F.C., F.R.S., joined the R.A.F. at the beginning of the war, became an air-gunner, then a navigator and eventually joined the staff at the Air Ministry.

'He was an amazing man. He was already an F.R.S. and a scientist of repute, and knew as much as most of the boffins who advised the Air Council, probably more. He used to drive them mad with his comments and criticisms, but he knew what he was talking about, and that's probably why they took him off flying,' said the man who was to become his pilot.

It didn't succeed altogether, because Wing Commander Jackson became the navigator for Squadron Leader Hartley on the series of trials they set up at night, against a Halifax bomber.

'Jackson was the sort of man who could bang the desk even with Air Marshals, though he had quite a low rank in com-parison. He was determined to keep the Junkers whole, so that it could be tried out by a crew who knew what it was like to be in the air at night, trying to shoot down the enemy. He got his way. I had a phone call telling me that it was on, and that he was going to be my navigator during the trials.

'The first one could easily have been the last, and not from any expected source. We could so easily have been shot down by our own Ack-Ack, or our own nightfighters.'

It was the first real test of the Lichtenstein's capabilities, and fitted in the plane for which it was intended, the Ju 88. The 'prey' was a Bomber Command Halifax from the Bomber Development Unit, with British radar, Ground Control Interception taking the role of the Wurzburg radar.

True, the Junkers *had* got British camouflage, it *had* got R.A.F. roundels on the fuselage and wings, easily recognizable in the daylight. But . . . it was still a Ju 88, and with the characteristic half-beat sound that the German unsynchronized engines made. The sound was enough to make any interested observer on the ground look up, identify the aircraft for what it was, and start pressing the Scramble button, for these trials were at night, and the R.A.F. identification letters would not be seen.

'Everything that could go wrong went wrong,' Squadron Leader Hartley recalled. The ground radar lost us on its screen. That wouldn't have been so bad, but then the V.H.F. set which linked us with the Halifax went u/s. It was a bit of a lash-up, and we had no way of contacting either the Halifax or the ground. We could hear them calling us, but we couldn't get through to them. There we were, stooging around the skies above England, in an enemy aircraft, unable to tell anybody who we were.

'I was tossing up in my mind what to do. I knew my own drome at Ford pretty well, and I reckoned that if I could get there, I could bang the plane down on the ground, jump out and start shouting before the guns opened up.

'But in the event, we did a bit of airfield hopping, keeping out of everyone's way until we got back to the base where they were expecting us. Wing Commander Jackson kept very quiet while we were in the air, but as soon as we landed, he let fly at everybody. It never happened again.'

Before the Junkers dropped, like Manna, from Heaven, the Fighter Interception Unit and its opposite number in Bomber Command, the Bomber Development Unit, had been co-operating already to try and find a method of shaking off the German nightfighters, drawn to them by the Lichtenstein radar. Squadron Leader Hartley, known as the man who would try anything, had already been playing the role of the German nightfighter, while Wing Commander Peter Cribb, a bomber Ace, did all he could to keep out of Hartley's way.

'I'd got a Beaufighter Mark 1 that I'd stripped everything out of, guns, seats, everything that would make it lighter. It was a sort of trials plane, completely stark, and with engines that my mechanics had tickled up. I reckoned that nothing could get away from me once I'd got that aircraft on its tail. Cribb and I had duels in the sky, me trying to get into a position to attack, and him trying to shake me off. But the objective was for him to get away, so we could compare notes even while flying, trying out manoeuvres that would shake me off. When we got the Junkers of course, it became that much better. It was *the* aircraft that was shooting down our bombers, and if Cribb could get away from me when I was flying *that*, we had a way of beating the Luftwaffe.'

Out of those mock duels between Cribb in the Halifax and Hartley in the Beaufighter and the Junkers came the one evasive manoeuvre which, as the German nightfighter pilots admitted after the war, could let the bombers off the hook. The 'corkscrew'. It became the standard method of shaking off a nightfighter, providing the reactions of the bomber pilot were fast enough, and he had room to manoeuvre. It took a very skilled fighter pilot to follow it.

As soon as the bomber pilot learned that the nightfighter was behind him, he put his aircraft into a dive for several hundred feet, and then, while the big plane was straining and the wings shaking, he would yank it back into a climb, and put even greater strains upon the engines and structure as they laboured to gain height, and at the same time bank the plane either to left or right.

If the nightfighter followed these moves, all made with speed so that he was taken by surprise, there was an even bigger surprise for him at the top of the bombers's climb, when its pilot cut the throttles so that the bomber came tumbling back on a reverse bank, with luck, right on top of the fighter chasing it.

The whole manoeuvre took place in about seven hundred feet of air, and wasn't an easy one to follow for any pilot, even Hartley.

'One of the first things I found out about the Junkers was that the vision on it was pretty bloody,' he said. 'The Beaufighters and Mosquitos had nice big screens that you could see out of, without craning. But though the Junkers was a beautiful aircraft to fly, much more manoeuvrable than the Beau or the Mosquito, it had a split windscreen, like the old pre-war cars, and that makes a great deal of difference when you're flying at night.

'At night, you can see much better on the periphery of vision, from the corner of the eyes. You don't look straight ahead, through the iris, you turn your head slightly to one side, so you can see out of the corner. With the split windscreen in the Junkers, I had to keep dodging from side to side, with my head turned slightly to one side anyway, to keep a visual on Cribb.

'And then we developed the "extended corkscrew", diving down, then climbing up fifteen hundred feet, banking at the same time, before throttling back and allowing the bomber to tumble.

'It was a beautiful counter, even more effective than the ordinary "corkscrew". It made it impossible for the fighter to get in a deflection shot as the bomber turned in front of me, and I was dodging from one side of the cockpit to the other. 'Then, when Cribb thought the moment was right, and I wasn't expecting it, he throttled back and fell back on me. The first time we did it, I was lucky to get the Junkers out of the way. We'd found the perfect counter to a nightfighter attack.'

There was a snag however, which meant it was never adopted, except by bombers on their own. A plane, in a bomber stream, using this manoeuvre and climbing fifteen hundred feet was likely to find himself mixing it with the bomber stream above him, and causing havoc to Bomber Command's timetable and the planes.

Hartley found another spin-off from the Junkers resulting from those tests.

The Lichtenstein radar, he discovered, sent out a very narrow-angled beam, only forty-five degrees, and even that hardly registered the all-wood construction of the Mosquito. So, after much badgering of the Air Ministry, he was given two Mosquitos to try out an experiment he thought would cause the Luftwaffe pilots to take a closer look at their life insurance policies.

'The planes already had a radar set in the nose, but we fitted a Mark IV set and aerial in the tail as well. Then we set out to "trail our coats" over Germany. At first the Air Ministry wouldn't let us mingle with the bomber streams, they would only let us go out on the nights when the bombers weren't operating, and we would go out and hope that someone would come up and fight, which they never did. By November 1943 though, we were being allowed to go out with the bombers, though we had other duties as well, like measuring the density of the bomber stream over the target. We were experimenting with the technique, finding what could be done with it.'

It took seven night flights, from June 29th, 1943, until July 13th, before Hartley and Jackson were satisfied that they had combed every bit of information from the Junkers that could be helpful to the bomber attack. At the conclusion, Hartley produced a report which told Air Chief Marshal Harris everything that could possibly be done to avoid the German nightfighters, the very information which the chief of Bomber Command had needed for so long to give his planes maximum effect at minimum risk.

In it, Hartley revealed that the Junkers had no vices, and compared very favourably with the Beaufighter in manoeuvrability, with deceleration rather slower than the Mosquito but greater acceleration. Its only handicap was the divided windscreen. Of the Lichtenstein radar, he reported that it was an efficient Aircraft Interception device, provided that the fighter could be kept pointed at the target aircraft. A weakness which the invention of 'corkscrew' exploited.

It proved itself on the last test, as Hartley reported.

'On July 13th the Halifax carried out extended corkscrews incorporating height change of fifteen hundred to two thousand feet, and a full power climb, the air speed indicator range being up to 240 m.p.h. Results were very much more encouraging, the visual being lost and the fighter being forced to break away. Lichtenstein contact was also lost in the move. In the early stages of the manoeuvre help was available from the Lichtenstein, but owing to the narrow coverage of the apparatus, all corrections were made to direct the fighter straight at the bomber, and if followed would have resulted either in an overshoot or a collision. On the only occasion when the fighter made a complete corkscrew satisfactorily, it ended up well below the bomber, and in attempting to attack from below in a steep climb was forced to break away when the bomber dived for the beginning of a second corkscrew.

'During this exercise the indications on the C.R.T.s (Lichtenstein screen) became poor on several occasions owing to the engines being throttled back. A run was therefore made with thirty degrees of flap, which resulted in improved Lichtenstein performance, but had an adverse effect on the directional stability and maneouvrability of the aircraft.'

More invaluable information for the bomber pilots to help them confuse their attackers. If they slowed down at the right moment, the only way the Junkers could prevent over-shooting them was to lower flaps to slow his own aircraft, and thus lose stability and manoeuvrability.

Schmitt told the R.A.F. that 70 per cent of the German Air Force Night Fighter Force were Me 110s fitted with Lichtenstein, and Hartley in his report was careful to make it clear that his conclusions could only relate to the Lichtenstein itself, or when it was fitted in the Junkers, a newer and better plane as a nightfighter than the Me 110, but of which only eleven were then left with the Luftwaffe.

Hartley continued in his report.

'From the results of the trials, it is clear that the Lichten-stein is an efficient A.I. (Air Interception – radar) for evasion-following. Its coverage limitations only seem important when the fighter cannot be pointed at the target without risk of overshooting, and those conditions will occur firstly in a diving orbit, and secondly in an extended corkscrew at two thousand five hundred feet range. Of the two manoeuvres, the latter is the harder to follow on Lichtenstein.

'The long-range diving orbit will result in loss of contact unless the rate of turn is controlled by pilot and operator act-ing in careful conjunction. The success of this manoeuvre therefore depends on the state of training of G.A.F. (German Air Force) crews. P.W. (Schmitt) stated that operators received no training on the Lichtenstein at base, and little subsequent practice in following violent evasion; practices were limited and mainly designed to exercise the Wurzburg operators. He pointed out that bombers usually flew straight and level, or with a gentle weave which created no problem, and he considered that the average crew would have grave difficulty in following an orbit even at ranges of less than five thousand feet. He stated however that the Wurzburg re-mained on the bomber until the interception was completed, and that if contact was lost in this manner, fresh vectors could soon be given.'

Schmitt's knowledge as a fighter pilot, given to then Squadron Leader Hartley over tea in an A.B.C. café enabled Hartley to be even more specific in his report. The Luftwaffe, he told Hartley, received theoretical instruction in deflection shooting, but no actual air firing or camera gun practice.

'Great emphasis is laid on the importance of surprise,' Hartley continued, 'and there is a tendency of pilots to disengage and attempt a fresh approach if the behaviour of the bomber indicates that the fighter has been spotted. The first turn of the corkscrew should therefore be made if possible towards the moon, with the object of getting clear of the fighter in the climbing turn, or alternatively of turning towards the fighter if he has already disengaged for a fresh approach. P.W. (Schmitt) also suggested that when no fighter was seen, fire should be opened from the rear turret in a general direction astern, and thirty degrees to forty degrees downwards, as he expected this would have a discouraging effect on the average G.A.F. crew.'

Schmitt also advised that since almost all attacks developed from below, the immediate action for any bomber in imminent danger of attack was a steep dive as this would force the fighter to disengage. This agreed entirely with Hartley's own opinion.

As his conclusion, Hartley recommended that the extended corkscrew should be adopted as the standard combat manoeuvre for night bombers, and that to achieve the best results against Lichtenstein, the extended corkscrew should be started at a range of three thousand to two thousand five hundred feet.

Except in the cases of bombers flying away from the bomber streams, and in single combat with enemy fighters, this recommendation was not adopted. When it was, it gave the bomber a fighting chance against the Junkers.

CHAPTER FOURTEEN

VIRTUALLY from the time of his arrival at the Fighter Interception Unit, Squadron Leader Hartley became its Commander, as the C.O. Wing Commander Simpson was on duty in America. He became the C.O. subsequently anyway, the leading experimenter in the R.A.F., a test-pilot not only of aircraft, but of any daring scheme put up by himself or anyone else, that might conceivably benefit the Allied cause.

When information filtered back to Britain through its network of spies on the Continent, that the Germans had been forced to fall back on visual and radio beacons as rallying points for their fighters, because the British interference with their radar system had been so successful, it was Hartley who went out to check if it was true.

'We were told that there was a beacon, a light in such and such an area, and I was asked, would I please go up there, and if it was there, what was happening. This I proceeded to do. It was there, all right, but so were a hundred German fighters. At that point my radar packed up.'

Nothing daunted, Hartley, as he put it, 'extricated himself' from the crowd of German aircraft, all circling the beacon, seeking nothing more than a British aircraft to shoot at, and unaware that one had joined their ring o' roses game.

Outside the circle, the radar behaved normally again, so Hartley joined the game once again, and again found that his radar went u/s. The Germans had found a way to jam the British airborne radar. As he was on an intelligence sortie, Hartley didn't hang around any longer and once again got out of the beacon area, and on his way home.

But that same night, while Hartley in his Mosquito with its backward facing radar was out, so were several other nightfighter Squadrons also fitted with his device, in a raid on Dusseldorf. A German nightfighter who crept up behind one of the Mosquitos, fully expecting to take it by surprise, and unaware that every move he made was being watched inside the aircraft on its backward facing screen, was shot down when the Mosquito made its sudden turn. The first victory of Hartley's technique.

Having proved the success of that technique, Hartley looked for other ventures.

'I normally put myself on every new job that came up. There were a number of blind-landing projects coming up, what we used to call blind approach, various beacons to be tested. And also, the first "head-up" display ever.

'It was a projection on the windscreen of the basic flying instruments so that at night, you didn't have to look inside the cockpit, you got a visual indication on the windscreen, so that you could fly on it. It didn't work. It was a wonderful principle, but it was far from operational at the time. But of course, now, it has been tremendously developed for civil aviation.'

Then, as the preparations for the Invasion began, Hartley and his Fighter Interception Unit began to get a number of odd jobs. One of them was to 'take-out' the German radar stations.

'Someone had discovered a device where, if you tuned into the right frequency, you could home in on the radar beam, follow it down and destroy the post. We were interested in those on the Channel coast obviously.

'The homer was fitted into a Typhoon, and we tried it out on a German Wurzburg up in Berwickshire, that had been captured in Sicily and brought back. All the homing worked jolly well, so that we went out to bust the radar stations on the French coast.

'But it didn't work. What happened was that in the preliminary trials, they realized what was happening and wouldn't play ball. Every time they saw us coming they switched off.

'The homer was so accurate that you could launch the rockets down it. The idea was I went in with it, marked the target with my rockets and a wing of Typhoons would come in from behind and finish it off. But I doubt if it worked more than twice before the Germans twigged, and switched their sets off

'But there were quite a lot of other odd-jobs going on at that time. We were trying out the Westland Welkin, a high-altitude fighter. It never went into production because the

106

need for it disappeared. It was the first high-altitude, really practicable high-altitude, fighter. I had it up to forty-three thousand feet, in a pressurized cabin. The Germans had got a very high-flying Ju 86 bomber, and the Welkin was the answer to it. But by the time it was ready for service, the Ju 86s had disappeared and never came back.'

Another of Hartley's odd-jobs was to find the best technique of shooting down Hitler's first Victory weapon, the V1, 'Flying bomb' which was launched during daylight and at night-time.

'We were given Tempests to see if we could use them at night against the "Flying bomb". The day Tempest squadrons were not *night*fighter pilots, they would have needed special training unless they wanted to kill themselves. We had very experienced nightfighter pilots and so we set to work. It proved a rather expensive operation, but it worked, when we had made every mistake we could.

'You could fly into the ground rather easily when you were chasing a V1, and I lost one chap that way. It was so easily done. I found trees going past once, and pulled up just in time. Another of my chaps was chasing a bomb when it flew into the side of a hill and blew up, but fortunately he was just far enough behind to be out of the way. The answer was that the bombs could fly so low, but they didn't have people in.

'Another one of my chaps shot one down, but didn't get out, I don't know what happened there. Another pilot made two or three forced landings at night, but got back to base each time. He'd been shooting at bombs which got too close to him, and blowing up the warhead, getting his own plane damaged in the explosion.

'But we proved the operation would work, and they formed a special Tempest Squadron to do it. I lost two people in it, and ended up in hospital. I ran into a Mosquito, or he ran into me, at night, when we were both manoeuvring after the same bomb. I had to get out rather smartly, parachuted down and broke a leg on landing. I wasn't fit for full flying for about nine months, it wasn't until after the end of the war that I was fully operational again, although I had a limited clearance and could fly light aeroplanes.'

Although on crutches, Squadron Leader Hartley continued commanding the unit, until the war in Europe ended.

CHAPTER FIFTEEN

THE three Luftwaffe men, this time in civilian clothes with an S.I.S. escort, caught the evening train from Aberdeen station the day after they landed, May 10th, where they continued disgorging the information which the R.A.F. sought so hungrily. They were given an escort of R.A.F. Regiment to the station, where Group Captain Colquhoun's responsibility for them ended. But it continued for the plane itself – and for the events for long afterwards.

It wasn't until May 14th that the Junkers 88 D5-EV, now wearing R.A.F. camouflage and roundels, and renumbered PJ 876 was flown to the Royal Aircraft Establishment at Farnborough for the series of tests by Squadron Leader Hartley and Wing Commander Jackson.

Dyce had seen eventful times in the intervening days. A Spitfire X.4334 of the Operational Training Unit on the airfield was reported overdue on a cross-country exercise, and at the same time a trawler in the Pentland Firth reported seeing a Spitfire crash into the sea three miles north of Thurso. It searched, but could find no trace of the plane or the pilot. But he had been able to get out of the crashed plane and into the dinghy. The cold water of the North Sea and a night in his sodden clothes was too much for the pilot, Pilot Officer R. J. F. Fiscaline, an Australian. His body was found in the dinghy the following day by the S.S. *Rota* and landed at Scrabster.

As preparations were made to fly the Junkers off, Pay parade was held on the drome, and a volunteer stood by the pay table to collect for the War Savings movement. Total collection was £118 1s. 0d.

And the following day, flight Lieutenant W. J. H. Childs of the R.A.F. Regiment and his thirty-two strong detachment which had manned the Ack-Ack guns that fired at the Junkers, and the picquet which guarded it subsequently, were transferred to R.A.F. Station, Langham. Group Captain Colquhoun made his customary round of inspections, visiting the Operations block, the Link Trainer section, the Met office and other adjacent buildings. On May 16th, another Spitfire X.4326 crashed near Fort William while on a training cross-country flight.

The business of Dyce had returned, almost, to normal. But Group Captain Colquhoun knew that storm clouds were gathering around his own head. The Air Ministry were looking for a scapegoat for the lack of security that had followed the Junkers' landing, and he had an uneasy feeling that he was to be it. He was expecting a visit from the Group Intelligence (Security) Officer. It came on May 26th.

May was an auspicious month for the British war effort, and as the warmth of the sun made the problem of finding sufficient clothes to keep warm one of how to make what clothes one had look like a new spring outfit, Britain began to rejoice at a succession of victories. One of the biggest of these was the Dambusters raid on the Moehne and Eder dams in the Ruhr, nineteen Lancasters with the special nine thousand pound bombs invented by Dr. Barnes Wallis, which attacked the Moehne, Eder, Sorpe and Schwelm dams.

Rehearsals for the raid had been going on for months, but it was information on the Fighter Defence system of the Reich, which Schmitt supplied, that enabled Bomber Command to plan the route across the Continent and back which helped the plan to succeed and brought eleven of the Lancasters back. Britain was getting the first fruits from the seed that the S.I.S. planted in the Luftwaffe in 1940. The monthly report prepared for the War Cabinet by the Chiefs of Staff of each service, telling of the armed forces successes and failures had much to say about the success of the Dambusters, but no mention was made of the even more important events at Dyce.

In the section on Home Security, the War Cabinet were told that during the first week of May 1943, daylight bombing and machine-gun raids had occurred on five days, and there had been two shelling incidents at Dover. On May 7th and 11th, Great Yarmouth and the nearby areas were attacked by bombers, causing considerable damage to houses in Great Yarmouth, dislocating railway services and damaging rolling stock. The raid on the 11th was on a military headquarters, in which bombs fell on A.T.S. billets killing twenty-six A.T.S. girls and twelve servicemen. During the week twenty-eight civilians were killed and twenty-two seriously injured.

Even the A.S.O. summary supplied for the Chiefs of Staff and the War Cabinet was circumspect in its reference to the incident. Nine German aircraft had made reconnaissances over the sea dividing the warring nations, and 'one of these aircraft made brief landfall over the Aberdeenshire coast'.

Schmitt, Rosenberger and Kantwill had been put well and truly under wraps. The less anyone knew about them, the better, the Secret Intelligence Service of the R.A.F. decided, and anyway there was plenty of other good news about without having to divulge this one until the time was right.

There was *bad* news for the Cabinet to hear. Three ships, which had been thought safely anchored in Gibraltar Bay were severely damaged by explosions below the water line – put there by the Italian human torpedoes. The Battle of the Atlantic was still going on, with an estimated one hundred and twenty U-boats in operation, but the shipping losses in April amounted to 313,000 tons – less than half the total for March. Because of the bad weather, only one large-scale attack was made by Bomber Command, on Duisburg on the night of May 12th/13th. It was successful, and large fires were started which made it impossible to photograph the following day because the smoke was so thick. But thirty-four of the five hundred and seventy-two bombers sent out failed to return. On the following night, four hundred and forty-four bombers were sent to attack the Skoda works at Pilsen, dropping four hundred and eighty-six tons of high explosive. Bomber Command sent out six hundred and ten aircraft on these two raids – thirty-three failed to return and two crashed in Britain. The percentage of losses was too high.

The American 8th Air Force with its daylight attacks made by its Flying Fortresses was faring better. In twelve raids on France and Germany in twelve days, it sent out a total of nine hundred and seventy-three aircraft for a loss of thirty-three – a high loss, but not as bad as the night bombers.

However, the North African campaign had ended, General Von Arnim, commanding the German troops, had been captured. Morale in Britain was rising, just as the morale in Germany was falling, where Goering had finally conceded that the Allies could bomb where and when they willed. Unable to find enough labour and materials to provide shelters for the German civilian population during air-attacks, he tried to convince them that slit-trenches were just as efficient, and on May 12th issued an announcement to the population.

'The Commander-in-Chief of the Luftwaffe has issued new rules for the construction of A.R.P. slit-trenches. Experience has shown that properly constructed slit-trenches offer particularly good protection and that trenches built of prefabricated sections of ferro-concrete give the best results. The construction of slit-trenches is to be furthered by all means, and the population is to be encouraged to take part in these self-aid measures. The Speer Ministry will take all necessary steps to provide building materials. A.R.P. slit-trenches are long, narrow, covered trenches which extend in zig-zag form. They must be constructed at some distance from buildings, parallel trenches must be at least twenty metres apart. No straight sector may be planned to give protection to more than fifty persons and no single trench, consisting of several sectors, may be planned to shelter more than two hundred persons. They are to be 1·40 metres wide and 1·95 metres high, covered by at least 0·50 metres of soil on top with banks of soil of 1·30 metres each. As far as possible, they are to be contructed below ground level.'

As the British morale rose, it was paralleled by an increasing confidence in the occupied countries. The civilians of Holland, Belgium and Denmark had always made a practice of ignoring the black-out regulations until virtually ordered at the point of a gun to turn their lights off, or black-out the windows. The practice spread even to Southern France, where Italian patrols walked the streets of the Riviera with orders to shoot at windows which were inadequately blacked-out.

At R.A.F. Dyce, Group Captain Colquhoun received the R.A.F. Group Intelligence Officer, a Squadron Leader, in his office, and explained the reasons for his actions on May 9th. He felt confident that he had acted correctly, and in the best traditions of the service. He was there when the plane landed and the crew got out of the aircraft, and it soon became apparent to him that the landing itself was highly confidential, needing utmost discretion.

He personally had seen to it that the prisoners were moved under escort, the Oberleutnant to the sick quarters, and the two other ranks to the guardroom's two cells. Although the three Germans all wanted to make statements on arrival, they were not interrogated until the arrival of the Air Intelligence (K) officer from the Group and the Senior Air Staff Officer.

He had the aircraft hidden as soon as possible as he was fearful that if the Germans had any suspicion it had landed at Dyce, they would send a reconnaissance aircraft over to take pictures as proof.

He had put a double guard on the aircraft all the time it remained at Dyce.

He had given a personal talk to all aircrew at 1200 hours on the following day warning them that there were special reasons why its landing should not be talked about as it was vital the knowledge did not get back to Germany, and the Senior Air Staff Officer of 14 Group had given a similar warning to the personnel of 165 Fighter Squadron. The Senior Air Staff Officer had also given a similar warning to the Press, and the Provost Marshal in Aberdeen had been asked to do all he could to stop the civil population talking about it.

Why had he not given a special warning to the whole camp, or taken other special security measures?

Group Captain Colquhoun explained that he felt that if he did so, everyone would realize that the arrival of the aircraft was of a particularly secret nature, and would be tempted to talk all the more. He hoped that the service personnel would be sufficiently security conscious to keep quiet about the incident. He hadn't enforced local censorship of letters because neither he nor the Intelligence Officer on the Station thought of doing so. It had slipped their memory.

On May 29th the Group Captain was asked to provide his own full explanation by the Air Vice-Marshal Commanding No. 17 Group. Once again he went over the ground, explaining how the plane's landing was so well known locally, even its make being identified by a civil policeman's son four miles from the aerodrome, that all he could hope for was that people would not recognize it as a nightfighter or in any way important, or that there was anything peculiar about the circumstances of its arrival.

'If I took special precautions, I was certain that someone at the very least would say outside, "we have been specially warned not to speak of this". Whereas if nothing was said the natural inference would be that the explanation was a normal one. i.e. that it was forced down by our fighters. I felt certain that any pronouncement would draw attention to their being a special feature in the case.'

Group Captain Colquhoun explained that he had not instituted any letter censorship because it would have been ineffective unless the whole Station was isolated. Some of the personnel, he pointed out, lived outside the camp, others in hostels and there were non-Service people who worked in the camp but went home in the evenings. The event was so widely known that those on the camp were a mere drop in the ocean.

His explanation was passed on to the headquarters of Coastal Command by the Group Commander with a covering letter stating that he considered all possible security measures had been taken, and that no blame could be attached to him for the leakage of information.

On June 11th, Group Captain J. Bussey from R.A.F. Benson took over command of R.A.F. Dyce, and Group Captain Colquhoun was posted to R.A.F. Uxbridge as a supernumerary.

CHAPTER SIXTEEN

THE job of evaluating the capabilities of the Junkers 88 and its Lichtenstein equipment could not have been given to three better men. The scientist, Dr. (now Professor) R. V. Jones, one of Britain's leading boffins during the war, now Professor of Natural Philosophy at Aberdeen University, was the originator of 'Window' and had been developing it since 1937. He had long advocated its use to help reduce the losses of bombers, and was very much on the side of 'Bomber' Harris, even to the extent of arguing forcefully with Prime Minister Winston Churchill at 10 Downing Street.

His entry in *Who's Who* reads like a page out of modern history, and occupies more than three-quarters of a column. At that time he was thirty-two, was educated at Alleyn's school, and Wadham College, Oxford, where he was an Exhibitioner, he took an M.A. at Balliol College, Oxford, and his Doctorate in Philosophy in 1934. For the two following years he was the Skynner Senior Student in Astronomy at Balliol before joining the Air Ministry as a Scientific Officer. in 1941 he was the Assistant Director of Intelligence.

Wing Commander Derek Ainslie Jackson, O.B.E., D.F.C., A.F.C., now Research Professor, Faculté des Sciences, Paris, was then thirty-seven, and married to the daughter of the second Baron Redesdale, the Hon. Pamela Freeman-Mitford. A highly controversial and forceful man, educated at Rugby and Trinity College, Cambridge, he had independent means and studied science as a hobby which enabled him to argue on equal terms and better with most scientists. Since the war he has had three other wives, one of them the widow of Prince Ernst Ratibor zu Hohenlohe Schillingfurst. He is now married to Marie-Christine, the daughter of Baron Georges Reille, and lives in France and Switzerland.

Squadron Leader Christopher Hartley, now Air-Marshal Sir Christopher Hartley, K.C.B., C.B., C.B.E., O.B.E.,

D.F.C., A.F.C., the son of Brigadier General Sir Harold Hartley, and now the Deputy Chairman of the British Hovercraft Corporation, was educated at Eton and Balliol College, Oxford. He was then thirty.

The day after the Junkers landed, Professor Jones, in London, was told of its arrival and what it contained, and caught the night sleeper from London for Aberdeen. He was told by Air Commodore Easton of R.A.F. Intelligence that it had landed, and asked if he would go up to Dyce to take charge of it.

'I arrived on the morning of the 11th, was met by an R.A.F. car at the station, and taken to Dyce,' he recalled. 'It was the Tuesday morning, and I went out to have a look at it. I had the covers taken off, and had a good look at it. It was still on the drome in the open, so I had it taken into a hangar out of the way of any German photographic reconnaissance plane. It was important that the Germans shouldn't know that we had the aircraft.'

Professor Jones and Wing Commander Jackson were old friends and associates, and had been involved together in many activities and undertakings to improve the planes of the R.A.F. and reduce the bomber losses. Jackson was one of the group surrounding the scientists who were endeavouring to convince Winston Churchill to allow the R.A.F. to use 'Window' and confound the German radar, and it was Jackson who was determined that the Junkers and its equipment should be kept whole so that it could be used in a series of experiments to test its effectiveness and efficiency. Professor Jones agreed, and in a telephone conversation they decided that the plane should be flown down to the Royal Aircraft Establishment at Farnborough and a series of tests undertaken.

'I'd talked to the crew several times,' the Professor recalled, 'and I suggested to the pilot that he might like to co-operate in the tests we were going to make. He was quite willing to fly the Junkers and match its performance and the effectiveness of the Lichtenstein against some of our bombers. He was quite looking forward to it.

'I'd made the arrangements for the plane to be flown down South and for it to be flown from the point of view of checking the radar, then Derek Jackson rang me up and asked who was going to fly the plane. But when I said that I'd fixed for the German pilot to do it, and that he'd agreed to fly it and so forth, Derek Jackson said "I don't want to fly with any bloody German, I want my own pilot." But I let myself in for a real broadside when I said, Is your pilot safe? "Christ man," he replied, "do you think I'd go up with him if he wasn't." '

Schmitt was, in fact, rather disappointed at not being allowed to help the British in assessing the Junkers' ability as a nightfighter, and his own as a pilot, but there was no gainsaying the point of view of Derek Jackson. Christopher Hartley became the pilot of the Junkers, and prepared the reports on the plane from the points of view of its qualities as a fighter plane, and as a radar interceptor.

'I'd never met Hartley before, but of course, I knew his father. He certainly wrote two very good reports, so impressive that I made it my business to find out who he was.'

The three men were quite dissimilar, R. V. Jones, a scientist, completely involved in the war of the ether before the war even started, and fully aware of the important part it would play in that war when it *did* start. Jackson, the scientist/pilot had a wild streak of irresponsibility, quite capable – as he proved on three occasions – of pulling a train's communication cord because he couldn't get a seat in a first-class compartment with his back to the engine. A man brought up in the lap of luxury whose twin brother had been killed in a sleigh accident before the war. Both brothers were physicists, who had enough money to treat physics as a hobby, do it for the fun of the thing and become acknowledged experts in their field. And Hartley, the ace pilot who could fly anything, one of the R.A.F.'s test pilots, able to take into the air planes fitted with the latest brainchilds of British scientists, bring them back and report with authority and knowledge on the equipment and how it affected the performance of the aircraft. The man with whom Wing Commander Jackson was prepared to trust himself in an untried enemy aircraft, and even more important, the man with whom he would trust the aircraft itself.

One of Professor R. V. Jones' first actions on returning to London was to recommend for decorations the two Spitfire pilots, Flight Lieutenant Roscoe and Sergeant Scaman. 'They should have got the D.F.C. for *not* shooting the Junkers down,' he said. 'I was so impressed with the restraint of these chaps in not opening fire, because we'd had photographic reconnaissance aircraft shot down by our own fighters, and I made very strong representations for them to get the D.F.C. for not shooting it down. But I think they got mentioned in despatches!'

A decoration for failing to shoot down an enemy aircraft seemed rather bizarre to the Air Ministry.

Professor Jones' interest in the metallized strips of paper that were codenamed 'Window' during the war, and that he had invented in 1937 to outwit the newly invented radar, were put before Professor F. A. Lindemann as early as 1938. Lindemann, later Lord Cherwell, the great friend of, and principal scientific adviser to Winston Churchill when he became Prime Minister, was as aware as Churchill that war with Germany was inevitable, and had long been campaigning for an increase in the British air force, and for money to be spent on scientific projects to defend the country. One of those he advocated in a minute to his friend Churchill in 1938 was the invention of the then Dr. R. V. Jones – 'Window'. But trials on it were never carried out.

'I was then developing infra-red,' said Professor Jones, 'and while other scientists were pointing out the weak points of infra-red, I was pointing out the weak points of radar, and this was the main one.'

Four years later, after a meeting with Lord Cherwell and Winston Churchill, in May 1942, 'Window' was almost used against the German radar. To the relief of 'Bomber' Harris, a plane was even loaded with the material – but it was called off at the last moment. Sir Sholto Douglas of Fighter Command was against it – and so was Wing Commander Derek Jackson, who convinced Lord Cherwell that the device would play havoc with Britain's own radar defences.

It wasn't until after Professor Jones had inspected the Lichtenstein radar on the Ju 88 that, in June 1943, he and Sir Robert Watson-Watt, the Chief of the team of scientists working on radar, and Jones' Chief, obtained an interview with Winston Churchill which had such dramatic results.

'There wasn't much doubt that it would be pretty disastrous on our own radar too, but we knew that the German

117

bombers were so completely tied up in Russia that they wouldn't be able to use it against us.'

Winston Churchill heard the two scientists put the case for using 'Window'. He had already heard the opinion of Lord Portal, the Chief of the Air Staff who had finally come down strongly on its side, and Sir Arthur Harris, head of Bomber Command had been pleading for its use ever since the Lichtenstein equipped nightfighters of the Luftwaffe had been decimating his bombers.

Churchill's answer was brief. 'Open the window'.

The final authority to use the material was given to Bomber Command on July 23rd, and the first 'Window' operation was against Hamburg on the night of July 24th/25th, 1943. It wasn't quite a one thousand bomber raid – Harris sent out seven hundred and ninety-one planes, but the German air defences were overwhelmed. The Wurzburg apparatus on the ground and the Lichtenstein radar in the nightfighters were rendered helpless.

Only twelve planes failed to return from the raid, a percentage figure of 1·5 – compared with the 6 per cent of the previous raids. 'Window' had proved itself.

CHAPTER SEVENTEEN

The boffin who arrived from London to take charge of the surrendered Junkers might have been a slim young man, but he had a lot of power. Not many people had the ear of that autocratic old man who had come to personify Britain, Winston Churchill, and Dr. R. V. Jones, the youngest of the trio who took over the plane, but still the leader, was one of them. He already had many friends on the Dyce Station. The Operational Training Unit of the Photographic Reconnaissance Unit was based there, and many of the pilots and instructors had flown missions for him over occupied territory and over Germany itself, bringing back pictures of the German radar installations which kept him up to date with the German progress in the war of the ether.

Jones made a quick assessment of the security situation in Aberdeenshire. There was no hope of keeping back the news that the Junkers had landed, that had already been distributed widely, and in fact, was known in London on the evening of May 9th. What *was* important was to keep secret the fact that it contained Lichtenstein equipment. Would it be best to keep quiet about it, allow speculation to run riot and hope that no-one came up with the right answer? Or should he take the Station into his confidence, tell them what it contained and rely on the security consciousness of the airmen and women to keep it to themselves?

Jones decided on the latter course, after talking with some of the P.R.U. pilots. He had the entire staff of the station assembled.

'I had all the pilots, the technicians and everybody else called together and I gave them an impromptu lecture on the German night defences, and what the importance of this aircraft could be from the point of view of countermeasures, and that the lives of the chaps in Bomber Command depended on this information not getting back to the Germans.

As a matter of fact it didn't get out at all. When I came back to Aberdeen and joined the University staff in 1946, the head of my workshop was also a former member of the Royal Observer Corps, and was a mine of information about everything that went on in the area during the war. One night we were talking, and he told me that one thing he had never found out was the truth behind the Junkers which had landed at Dyce in 1943. I told him then, and I was glad that I had taken the decision to confide in the station three years earlier. It was one of those occasions when treating everybody responsibly paid off. The Observer Corps knew the plane had landed of course, but they never learned the story behind it.'

Squadron Leader Hartley began the trials of the Junkers on June 14th, when, as the daily log of the Fighter Interception Unit recorded, 'Squadron Leader Hartley went to Wittering in the Hurricane and flew a big, fat Ju 88'. They were just to get the 'feel' of the plane, but even while getting used to the aircraft, Hartley and a Wellington from the Bomber Demonstration Unit, engaged in mock battles in daylight. Then on June 20th he and Jackson began the series of tests at night, which resulted in a report being prepared for the eargerly waiting hands of 'Bomber' Harris and his Command.

The effectiveness of the lessons learned during the trials Hartley had been conducting came to light after the war, when a number of German nightfighter aces were interviewed. All of them considered the corkscrew a most effective evasive manoeuvre, but more effective for the Lancaster than the twin-engined Halifax bomber, which was an easier target. However, when caught, the Lancaster caught fire more easily than the slower, but more robust Halifax.

German fighter technique was to follow the corkscrewing bomber through one complete movement which enabled them to anticipate the change of direction, and attack at the top of the movement. But if their cannon shells did not go home then, the experienced pilots would break away altogether and seek an easier target, or wait for a time, as they thought a second attack on the bomber would be suicidal.

But that was before 'Window', and its real qualities were discovered, and before the British bombers were fitted with another radar device to give a shock to attacking fighters, codenamed 'Serrate'.

Wilhelm Johnen was a nightfighter pilot in Holland the night the British bombers obeyed Churchill's order, and 'opened the Window'. At that time, in great secrecy, eight hundred and fifty tons of the metallized strips had been stock-piled in various bomber stations throughout the country. They measured thirty centimetres by one and a half centi-metres, were arranged in piles of five hundred side by side, with cardboard faces to protect them in handling, and were tied with a piece of string around the bundle. Every one of the bombers on that first raid was given its load of 'Window' in addition to its bombs, and given the instruction to start dropping the material at the rate of one bundle a minute as soon as it reached the position 54 degrees 34N 07 degrees 55E, and continue doing so until reaching 54 degrees 10N and 0720 degrees E on the return journey. For the first time, the aircraft were instructed to take the minimum evasive action, and to fly as high as possible. It was a triumph.

Johnen and the other nightfighters took off to intercept the bomber streams when they were reported to be over Northern Holland, but from then on, everything went hay-wire. No-one knew what was happening, and the British radio-interception radio stations, monitoring the conversa-tion and reports of the German fighter pilots were in hysterics of laughter as they listened to the German confusion.

'Many hostiles, many hostiles. Flying singly,' reported one pilot to his ground control, as the beam from his Lichtenstein radar bounced back from the descending strips of silver paper. 'Very many hostiles. It is impossible, too many hos-tiles,' reported another, who balked at the idea of attacking what appeared to be thousands upon thousands of bombers attacking Germany in a stream. Yet another, ordered in to the attack radioed back : 'Wait awhile, there are many more hostiles.'

Johnen in his own fighter, could feel the confusion spread-ing among his own ground control. The reports they gave seemed to be hurried and contradictory. One moment, the enemy seemed to be over Amsterdam, the next they were over Brussels. He could get no help from his own control, and decided instead to fly straight to Amsterdam. When he got there, all the other pilots were reporting radar contact with the bombers, but no-one knew where they were. Then his own radar operator reported a contact at fifteen thousand feet on his Lichtenstein. Three or four bombers heading for the Ruhr. Johnen hoped he would have enough ammunition in his aircraft to deal with them.

He settled himself ready for the attack, and was then confused with a hurried scream from his Lichtenstein operator, 'Bomber coming for us at a Hell of a speed, two thousand yards, fifteen hundred yards, five hundred yards. Where is he?'

Disconcerted, afraid that he had narrowly missed being collided with, and ashamed at not having been able to deal with the bomber, Johnen concluded that he had been near-missed by another fighter, there could have been no other explanation for the speed with which it appeared on the radar screen, and then vanished. His radio operator reported another contact – and exactly the same thing happened. No sooner did it appear on the Lichtenstein than it headed towards them at an amazing speed . . . and then vanished.

But while Johnen and the other defenders of Germany were jigging about wastefully over Amsterdam, the bomber stream had been heading steadily for Hamburg, and reached it with little disturbance, trailing its stream of Christmas decorations behind it. The plea for aid which the ground defences sent up was 'Calling all nightfighters, calling all nightfighters. Full speed for Hamburg. A thousand enemy bombers over Hamburg. Full speed for Hamburg.'

By the time the fighters arrived there, Hamburg was blazing, burning like a furnace, obvious for miles to the chastened nightfighters who had been drawn away by a feint, while the British delivered a crushing blow to the ribs. There was no Ack-Ack fire when they arrived to indicate the presence of the bombers. There was no need for it, they had been and gone.

Harris left Hamburg to burn, and sent his bombers out the following night with a new target – Essen. Exactly the same thing happened. The Ack-Ack guns and searchlights, dependent upon the Wurzburg radar to give the position of the bombers wavered uncertainly in the sky. The officers in charge of the radar berated their men, and were in turn berated for inadequacy. What chance had they of detecting a radar reflection on a bomber when the radar screens were filled with reflections? Of the seven hundred and five bombers sent out, twenty-six failed to return – 3·7 per cent, higher than the casualty rate on Hamburg – but still much lower than the average losses between April and June 1943, the frightening 5·3 per cent.

Just as Hamburg began to breathe again, Harris sent the bombers back again. On July 27th he despatched seven hundred and eighty-seven bombers against the city, losing only seventeen – 2·16 per cent of his bomber force, and two nights later, on July 29th another big raid, seven hundred and seventy-seven bombers went out, leaving twenty-eight behind. On three alternate nights, two thousand, three hundred and fifty-five bombers dropped seven thousand tons of bombs on the city. Hamburg was a wreck. The cost to Britain's bomber forces was fifty-seven planes.

The holocaust in Hamburg was not quite a Dresden, but very near it. The fires caused by the incendiary bombs were fed by a high wind which spread the flames everywhere, and in turn created even higher winds. Everything that could burn burned. Temperatures reached one thousand degrees. The draught caused by the vacuum as the intense heat rushed up to the sky was strong enough to tear large trees out of the ground which in seconds became ashes. Those people who took refuge in the air raid shelters were suffocated. Forty thousand people died. Another forty thousand were injured, and nine hundred thousand people were made homeless. The morale of Hamburg was broken, and the warning of what was to come spread to the other German cities. Germany began to despair and talk of capitulation, but the thought was never in Hitler's mind. On August 2nd, Harris sent another seven hundred and forty bombers to Hamburg to administer the *coup de grâce*. In those raids, three thousand block-busters, one thousand two hundred land mines, twenty-five thousand H.E. bombs and three million incendiaries as well as phosphorus bombs were dropped. Hamburg was dead.

Major J. B. Mullock of the Royal Artillery took over the position of the mid-upper gunner in a Lancaster of No. 5 Group operating from Bardney on the Hamburg raid of July 27th.

He was the Flak officer of the group, and wrote a report on the anti-aircraft defences of the city.

'We were in the last wave of the attack, and the fires at Hamburg were visible long before we reached the target area,' he wrote. 'The defences of Kiel were in action, heavy and light guns were co-operating with searchlights though no real "cones" were observed. When some thirty miles from the target it was evident that vast portions of the town were in flames which lit the sky for miles around. We approached the target from the NE flying straight and level at twenty-two thousand feet – bombs were dropped at 01.32 hours.'

Hamburg, he reported was a remarkable sight, the town appeared to be ablaze, and although his aircraft was flying at twenty-two thousand feet, a huge column of smoke towered above them, reaching up to about twenty-four thousand feet, and making it impossible for the probing fingers of the searchlights to find the aircraft which were raining bombs.

But the success of the bombers in itself presented a problem, Major Mullock pointed out. As his own plane bombed, he counted fifteen other bombers silhouetted against the fires below, an easy target for any German fighters which might have been patrolling over the city. But, like the first 'Window' raid of July 24th, the nightfighters had been thrown into confusion by another trick; 'Spoof' raids upon other cities, where 'Window' was dropped, but no bombs, so that the ground defences did not know from which direction to expect the attack and which town was to be the victim.

The success of 'Window' was greater even than anticipated, and lived up to the expectations of Professor R. V. Jones. The losses in raids on German targets had been cut by more than a third, and the number of attacks on bombers by German fighters reduced by half, both effects at times when past experience made it likely that the rates would rise.

German anti-aircraft guns were also only achieving half their previous success, and the first raid taught the British a number of lessons which they introduced on each succeeding raid. It was, for instance, undesirable for isolated aircraft to fly higher than the main concentration – they lost the protection offered by the main drop of 'Window'. Because the

Stirling bomber flew so much lower than the Lancasters, and the effectiveness of 'Window' lasted only about five thousand feet, it was important not to have them follow directly behind the four-engined plane unless they were accompanied by the Halifax, or Wellington, or both, which were able to give the slower and lower Stirling protection with their own 'Window' screens.

The raids upon Germany and Italy, with the bombers hidden behind their protective screens went on through July, and then August. Remscheid was attacked by two hundred and seventy-three bombers on July 30th, Milan on August 7th; Mannheim August 9th; Nuremburg August 10th; Milan and Turin on August 12th; Milan again on August 14th; Turin August 16th; Peenemunde with five hundred and ninety-seven bombers on August 17th, when forty bombers failed to return and the loss rate went back above the pre-'Window' average – 6.7 per cent.

What had happened was that, protected by 'Window', Bomber Command could now take on targets that were the most heavily defended in Germany; targets that it had previously considered unwise to attack. Peenemunde was such a one, and the night chosen to attack it was one when there was bright moonlight, and the bombers were easily silhouetted; Lichtenstein was not needed, they could be attacked by visual means alone.

From July 24th until the end of August, seven thousand, five hundred and ninety-five bombers took part in the raids upon the Axis countries. Of them, two hundred and twenty-three aircraft were lost – a high figure but still only 2·95 per cent.

Lord Portal, Chief of the Air Staff wrote to Winston Churchill on August 30th, and gave him the good news about the success of the new device. It was the busiest ever month for Bomber Command, he told the Prime Minister, a total of six thousand, three hundred and twenty planes being sent out, April having been the previous best with six thousand and eighty-two sorties. For the fifth consecutive month the weight of bombs dropped broke all previous records, sixteen thousand, eight hundred and thirty tons of bombs being dropped – fifteen thousand, three hundred and fifty-eight of them on Germany.

Although 'Window' hadn't been introduced until July 24th, the casualty figures for the month were quite low at 3·7 per cent, which, Portal explained, was due to the surprise achieved on the Cologne raid of July 8th, and the weather conditions being against German fighters on the Gelsen-chirchen raid of July 9th. Portal was quick to point this out, and to give the credit for the low casualty rate on the raids towards the end of the month to 'Window'.

As the Germans got over their early surprise, a rise in the casualty figures even on the 'Window' raids had to be expec-ted, he warned Churchill, but even then, it would still be less than before the device was introduced.

Churchill, never a man to spare more words than he could help, sent a memo back. It contained the one word – 'Good', signed W.S.C.

Churchill's pleasure and growing confidence spread throughout the Cabinet, through his Chiefs of Staff and Ministers, and then gradually, throughout the country. He compared Portal's latest report with one which the Chief of Air Staff had sent him in May giving him the bombing figures for that previous best month of April, when a then record weight of eleven thousand, four hundred and sixty-five tons of bombs were dropped.

The losses of bombers then were 5 per cent, while the famous 'Pathfinders', whose job it was to pinpoint the targets with incendiaries, to make the task of finding the targets easier for the main bomber force had gone up as high as 8·7 per cent for the Pathfinder Stirlings.

April, Portal had concluded, had shown a very satisfactory increase in effort, but he added, 'it is clear that the rapidly increasing strength of the enemy defences is making the task of Bomber Command more expensive. In these progressively more arduous conditions the Lancaster shows up to great advantage over the Stirlings and Halifaxes.'

But to keep the bomber offensive going, the Stirlings and Halifaxes had to be used. Portal had struck a sombre note with that warning, adding as he had that the losses in the month of April were the highest since December 1942, higher than the average of the past twelve months, and likely to go higher as the summer approached, the effort was directed against more important and thus more heavily defended tar-

126

gets, the nightfighter force of the enemy increased and the density and depth of his ground radar improved.

Churchill compared the two reports and was glad that he had given the order to 'open the Window'.

CHAPTER EIGHTEEN

Not all 'Window' was dropped over Germany. Some bomber crews, in a mood of abandon, their mission accomplished, unscathed and back over the English countryside, were not beyond dumping their unused material down the chute, leaving it to flutter down and irritate the British farmers. It upset them just as much as it did on the Continent, where the German radio was deliberately fostering the impression that the device was poisonous to cattle and pets.

Nobody much minded when the Danish radio broadcast a warning to the public, that a lot of tinfoil had been dropped in the Haderslev district, which previous experience had shown, was poisonous to cattle. But the mutterings of the British farmers were focused into a roar when some 'Window' found its way on to the land of Lord Stanhope. He talked to other farmers, found out that they too had been affected, and penned a letter to his old friend Sir Archibald Sinclair, the Air Minister. After all, agriculture was also an important item in the British war effort.

'Dear Sinclair, I wonder if you would persuade your Air Boys to refrain from dropping the silvered paper (which I believe they carry to obviate German radio-location) when flying over this country. Lately we have been sprinkled with strips such as the one which I enclose. As they are coated with metal substance to catch the radio, these strips will, of course, not disintegrate like ordinary paper, and when they are swept up in the hay or other crops, they are not going to do young cattle any good. Nor will it help threshing. I rather think that on their way home the airmen lightheartedly throw this stuff out. Anyhow, there is a good deal of it about, and frankly, we farmers do not like it. Yours sincerely, Stanhope.'

This *was* serious, and Sir Archibald Sinclair ordered an immediate investigation. The culprits were never found, but strict warnings were sent to all bomber groups, and eventually, Lord Cherwood sent a placatory letter to the farming peer.

There was other damage caused by the jettisoning of 'Window' over Britain which indicated the side-effects it could be having on occupied territory. The B.B.C.'s Hull transmitter, and the electricity grid system over a wide area were put out of action when some of it was dropped by a low-flying bomber over Hull. Even more serious than dropping it over farmland. The Air Ministry sent a telegram to Bomber Command H.Q. warning of the danger to life if the metal strips became suspended from overhead cables, apart from taking the B.B.C. off the air.

The dropping arrangements for the material were primitive. Because of the need for secrecy, trials were kept to a minimum, and the few that *were* made worked successfully. The bundles were dropped, by hand, through the flare chute of the Halifax aircraft, and spread widely before dropping gently to the ground. But on the first 'Window' operation on July 24th, some of the bundles didn't open, and it was found their behaviour pattern varied from aircraft to aircraft. In the Wellington bomber, the problem was overcome by providing a cord with one end fastened to the plane, and the other hooked to the cord around the bundle. When the cord reached its limit of travel, the string broke and the parcel emptied. All this had to be done by a member of the crew, in addition to his normal duties, not always easy when the plane was under attack, the pilot had gone into a corkscrew manoeuvre, and the unfortunate crew member was being thrown from one side of the cabin to the other, while still trying to play his part in keeping up the defensive 'Window' screen.

But they *did* work. The strips, cut to a length equal to about half the wavelength of the German Wurzburg and Lichtenstein radar, were more or less tuned to that particular station, and resonated electrically when in that particular field, re-radiating part of the energy they received. While able to produce spurious signals on the enemy radar, it had little or no effect on the British sets. They were packed in bundles of two thousand, and the response produced by one bundle when emptied was equal to that given by a single aircraft. It fell at about three hundred feet a minute. On

July 24th, the first night, fifty tons were dropped, commencing twenty miles North of Heligoland on the journey to Hamburg, and ending about twenty miles West of Heligoland on the return. Altogether one hundred and twelve thousand bundles were dropped which gave the same effect as one hundred and twelve thousand aircraft. No wonder the Wurzburg controllers went berserk.

The Secret Intelligence Service brought back the news that the officer in charge of one Wurzburg was mad with rage at his inability to find the bombers on his screen, and was heard to declare that he would rather be bombed by one hundred aircraft than submit to the flood of paper that confused his radar screen. He had detected seven hundred machines, and hadn't been able to locate one of them.

It wasn't so for the bombers. They fired at a number of fighters which they found either on their own radar screens or saw visually, whilst the Germans were still vainly trying to find them. Of the twelve lost on that first raid, three were shot down on their way to the target, five over the target and four on the return journey.

Although Germany had its own 'Window', no-one had carried out the order Hitler had given at that meeting in July 1942; to develop a way of countering it if the British did use it, and cause the destruction of the German Ground Control Interception system. Someone had to take the blame, and General Kammhuber, the A.O.I.-in-C. Nightfighters, who had been responsible for the construction of the German defence system was sacked. He was replaced by General Josef Schmidt – known to his subordinates, though never in his hearing, as 'Pepi' Schmidt.

It wasn't until some time had passed that the German associated the paper strips which littered the countryside with the breakdown of their radar system, and these bits of metallized paper proved to be just as indigestible to the German cattle as they were to those of Lord Stanhope and the Danish farmers. The rumour grew, helped along by British sympathizers and agents, that the Allies were dropping paper coated with arsenic in order to poison the countryside, and police, equipped with special protective gloves, were detailed to collect it. The rumour was so persistent that British scientists in the Government Laboratory were asked to make a analysis of 'Window' strips in case, inadvertently, they did contain poisonous material. But none was found. It was, however, another worry for Germany and the German population.

The euphoria which surrounded the success of 'Window' – everyone in the R.A.F. was now a confirmed supporter of long-standing – made the early battles to get it used a part of history. The Chiefs of Staff and the Directorate of Bomber Operations had pushed for it on the grounds that :

(a) it was imperative to stem the increasing tide of bomber losses, and 'Window' as a countermeasure to German radar defence seemed to offer the best means of doing this.

(b) although once used, it couldn't remain a secret, as our radar operated on a longer wavelength than that of Germany, it would be a much more difficult device to use against us.

(c) the German bomber strength was on the decline, whilst that of the Allies was increasing, so it would be of more value to the Allies than Germany. In any event, the German Air Force was being forced to devote first priority to the Russian and Mediterranean fronts.

(d) it was inconceivable anyway that the Germans hadn't thought of such a simple way to interfere with radar equipment.

Against these arguments, the scientists and Fighter Command took the view that :

(a) if the enemy retaliated by using the same material, our whole defence system would be in danger.

(b) it would be more prudent to wait and see what the outcome of the Russian campaign was.

(c) the British bomber losses had not been appreciably increased.

(d) Britain should wait until it had a counter to 'Window'.

(e) it wasn't expected that its use would save more than 0·5 per cent of the British bombers.

(f) Germany had developed a backward-looking radar similar to that of the British 'Monica' for use on her night bombers. If they used this and their equivalent of 'Window', the efficiency of the British fighter system would be cut by at least 80 per cent.

Many people had forgotten the long drawn-out arguments

131

before Bomber Command was allowed to introduce the device which cut its bomber losses by more than half. Many people, but not Air Marshal Harris.

On August 6th, 1943, the Air Ministry sent him a letter detailing what it thought should be done to improve the use the bombers got from 'Window'. In a long rigmarole, it drew attention to what Harris already knew, and had long been advocating.

'Sir,

I am directed to inform you that in view of the marked success which has attended the initial employment of "Window" in bombing operations, it is considered that all possible technical and tactical measures should be taken immediately to exploit it to the full. Continued success would not only increase the morale, efficiency and striking power of our bomber force, but would at the same time react adversely upon the confidence and morale of the enemy defences.'

Then followed paragraph after paragraph of a Scientific Intelligence report on the early German reaction to 'Window', which Harris had already received, that had been discussed at the Air Ministry who offered suggestions upon it.

Finally, the letter asked Harris to ... 'undertake urgently a close examination of all means of exploiting, and if possible, improving the new tactical situation which "Window" has brought about ...'

Harris tore the letter apart in detail.

'Sir, I have the honour to refer to your letter of 6th August, 1943, regarding the employment of "Window" in bombing operations. I fully appreciate the importance of determining the best tactical use of this countermeasure in association with other devices. A careful study of the tactics to be employed with this countermeasure was made prior to the first operation, and the results obtained have since been continually under review with the object of ensuring that operational plans are so made as to obtain the maximum efficiency from "Window".'

Then, paragraph by paragraph, he pointed out that he had been stating the obvious for more than a year, and needed no help from newcomers to the bandwagon. A lot of bomber crews had been lost in that year.

Although the July 24th raid on Hamburg was the first

official use of a device to throw German radar off the scent, disquieting reports reached the Air Ministry of *unofficial* experiments that took place long before. A Secret Agent reported from Germany in 1942 that a British bomber had deceived a German control station by throwing out aluminium dust, and then changing its altitude. As the cloud of aluminium dust was nearer the control radar than the plane, the radar beam followed the dust, and guided the German nightfighters in that direction, who even opened fire upon the cloud. The bomber meanwhile had escaped behind its own original ancestor of 'Window'.

But there were logistics attached to 'Window' which no-one had taken into consideration. The supply of aluminium with which the paper was coated. Bomber Command thought in terms of ten major raids a month, which meant four hundred and fifty tons of 'Window' had to be manufactured, which in turn required one hundred and fifty tons of aluminium. Multiplied by twelve it meant losing the equivalent of two hundred and fifty Lancasters or eighteen hundred Spitfires a year. Air Chief Marshal Sir W. R. Freeman, the Chief Executive of the Ministry of Aircraft Production put it tersely, in a letter dated April 11th, 1943, when the success of 'Window' was still being estimated, and before the Ju 88 had arrived, 'By using the foil you save aircraft and crew – you lose more aircraft off production than you save.'

Fortunately, the Jeremiahs were proved wrong, not least by the savings in bombers, much bigger than even the greatest advocates of 'Window' dared hope, brought about by the countermeasures.

CHAPTER NINETEEN

'WINDOW' wasn't the only contribution that the Lichtenstein, the Junkers 88 and its crew had to make to the British war effort. There was a great deal more mileage to come out of it and them, even pressure from the American Air Force through the R.A.F. Delegation in Washington in June 1943 to send the Lichtenstein equipment to America for their scientists to experiment with, turned down out of hand by the Air Ministry.

'Very much regret we cannot send you A.I. (Air Interception) equipment since it is the only one so far available, and it is in continued demand for urgent tests. Hope however to be able to comply as soon as we get a duplicate. In the meantime I will see the fullest technical details are sent to you as soon as possible.' But it was some time before the R.A.F. got another example of the Lichtenstein, whole.

By March 1944, the Ju 88, brand-new when Schmitt delivered it to Dyce, had been so much engaged in experimental work that the British mechanics could no longer keep the plane flying, and it was pronounced as beyond repair. The Lichtenstein lived on, transferred into a Beaufighter and on April 24th, the tests continued.

Schmitt and Rosenberger were also kept busy. One of Schmitt's first acts on reaching London was to broadcast over the English radio station 'Gustav Siegfried eins', the German language station beamed at Germany. To listen to it was a treasonable offence, punishable by death, but by arrangement, Schmitt's father tuned in on May 13th, and after the introductory flourish of trumpets, and the announcement 'Hier spricht der Chief' heard the code message, 'Der Mai ist gekommen' – May has arrived. He knew his son had reached England.

'Gustav Siegfried eins' was an important weapon in the British armoury, and had the same attraction for the German population as the 'Gaarmany calling' of William Joyce, 'Lord Haw Haw', the Briton who joined the German cause and broadcast propaganda back to Britain. Its purpose was the same, to undermine morale, and contradict the normal broadcasts. The British had refined it to an extent that even Lord Haw Haw couldn't compete with.

They had an actual fighter pilot, addressing by name his former colleagues in his old squadron, calling upon them to desert.

'The war is lost,' he broadcast to them, 'don't sacrifice your lives for a futile war and incompetent leaders. In England and Sweden there are airfields where you will be welcomed as we were. Remember – waggle the wings of your aircraft, and you will be escorted in to a safe landing.'

To the credit of the German pilots, there are no records of Schmitt's advice being taken.

Schmitt and Rosenberger became regular broadcasters on the R.A.F. programme which the B.B.C. sent out at 4.0 p.m. each day on the 373 metres wavelength, the 1500 metres wavelength; two wavelengths in the 41 metres band, five wavelengths in the 31 metres band; five wavelengths in the 25 metres band and one wavelength in the 16 metres band. It lasted for fifteen minutes, included a B.B.C. news bulletin – and more important for the listeners in Germany, who couldn't help tuning in despite the punishment for those who were caught – news of missing German Air Force crews.

They co-operated with British script-writers in preparing talks which emphasized British superiority, but which would arouse the interest of the Luftwaffe crews and lessen their morale. They discussed technical matters, gave summaries of British operational achievements with details of bomb damage on target cities, and even gave descriptions of the Allied planes against which the Germans were flying, the Thunderbolts, Mosquito and Typhoon. They gave descriptions of the German's own aircraft, comparing their performance with the comparable Allied types, underlining how hopeless the task of the fighter pilots would be if they found themselves faced with one in an air duel.

Schmitt in one broadcast, told his former comrades :

'In 1942 the German Air Force put into service only three really new types. These were the Focke Wulf 190, the

Henschel 129 and the Messerschmitt 210. Apart from these three, the German Air Force has only improved former types, some of them have certainly been considerably improved.

'Of the three new types, the Focke Wulf 190 comes first, an excellent fighter, for which the Royal Air Force has every respect. With its heavy armament and good rate of climb this machine has so far given a good account of itself. The Focke Wulf 190 has often been used also for nuisance raids on England. But for this purpose the machine did *not* turn out very practicable. Although these sneaking raids are only three or four minutes on an average over our coastline, yet their total of losses is very high. Last winter every eighth German nuisance raider was brought down over the English coast, a loss of $12\frac{1}{2}$ per cent.'

Depressing news for the German pilots who had to undertake the raids.

Schmitt went on to criticize the Henschel 129, a ground-attack aircraft which was, he said, excellent, but which depended so much on good fighter protection. The Messerschmitt 210 had made two appearances over England, but as both had been shot down by Typhoon fighters, their qualities were doubtful. And he reminded them of other wonder machines which had been launched with big build-ups in the German newspapers, but which had quietly disappeared, planes like the Messerschmitt 323. During the Tunisian campaign an entire formation of thirty-one of these aircraft had been shot down into the sea.

He talked about conditions in Prisoner of War camps, even going into detail about individuals, airmen who had been shot down.

'Soldat Karl Sahm had to be admitted to hospital with malaria, but is now fully recovered and has been discharged. Oberfeldwebel Kurt Diecke, whose parents Otto and Marie Diecke live in Elsterwerda-Biebla, Am Steim, had to be taken to hospital with two broken ribs after he had been captured, but has now been discharged from hospital, completely recovered.'

Important though the Air Ministry considered these broadcasts to be, there were even more important broadcasting duties for Schmitt and Rosenberger which had a more direct effect upon the Luftwaffe, and which probably caused more annoyance to the Germans than all the other British radio countermeasures put together. Operation 'Corona'.

With its Ground Control Interception baffled by the 'Window' strips, and with 'Tinsel', the jamming device used by the British bombers interrupting the control of the fighter-aircraft from the ground, the German ground control let their nightfighters freelance, able only to give them a running commentary on their high-frequency radios of the state of play in the air above, and where the British bombers were thought to be heading. But even this sole link was capable of interruption, and the British interrupted it.

A high-power ground radio transmitter was built and was controlled from the British listening station at Kingsdown, operating on the same radio frequency as the German radar controllers used to give their running commentary.

The 'Corona' transmitter could be tuned to the precise frequency of the German broadcast in something less than two minutes, and then Schmitt, Rosenberger and other German-speaking operators began causing confusion in the air above Germany. Having spent so much time involved in the actual conversations they were then sending-up, Schmitt and Rosenberger were particularly successful in creating chaos. They even recognized some of the voices of the controllers, as *they* issued instructions which Schmitt and his wireless operator promptly contradicted.

The German nightfighter pilots did not know whom to believe. On the night of November 17th, the 'Corona' operator issued a general instruction to all nightfighters to land immediately. They did, ignoring the hysterics of the real ground control, vainly trying to direct them against the attacking bombers. Then, on another raid on October 22nd, after a verbal duel with the German control issuing one set of instructions, promptly countermanded by the 'Corona' broadcaster, the German controller told his planes 'not to be led away by the enemy' and ordered them all, in the name of General Schmidt to obey his instructions. 'Corona' won the duel on the night of the Mannheim raid on November 17th, and caused absolute confusion in the German operations room. Orders given to the fighter aircraft were immediately countermanded, and 'Corona' warned the fighters of fog, bringing a reaction from the German controller to ignore that instruction, 'The fellow blinding about the fog is English'. Nevertheless he ordered the aircraft to land immediately afterwards.

By February 1944 the German nightfighter commander, 'Pepi' Schmidt had devised new methods of ensuring that the orders of his radar controllers would be in no doubt, and 'Corona' stopped its back chat war, becoming another jamming station, sending out a garbled mixture of voices on a recording which did nothing to help the German pilots.

In October, Lord Portal the Chief of the Air Staff reported to Churchill that although only four thousand, six hundred and eighty sorties were sent out, the lowest number since January, dropping only thirteen thousand, seven hundred and seventy-seven tons of bombs – all but ninety-three tons on Germany – the rate of loss was still below the average rate for the previous twelve months, thanks to the introduction of 'Window'. The defence system which it had forced the Luftwaffe to adopt was vulnerable to diversionary and spoof attacks, and the effectiveness of the jamming methods used by the R.A.F. was increasing.

The following month's report contained the news Churchill wanted to hear. Sir Arthur Harris and his Bomber Command had begun the bombing offensive against Berlin. During November two thousand bombers were sent out to the German capital, and dropped six thousand, nine hundred and ninety tons of bombs on it. It cost eighty-four aircraft, 4 per cent casualties – high, but still lower than the figure Bomber Command would have expected in a raid on the heavily defended prime city had not the bombers been shielded by the metallized strips of paper, 'Window'.

While the bomber offensive gained strength, there was yet another dividend paid by the Ju 88 which was still being used in trials even as the first 'Window' raid on Hamburg in July 1943 was taking place. In order to locate the bombers, the Lichtenstein equipment on the nightfighter had to send out a strong signal, and it was possible to home on that signal if all the technical details on the radar were at hand. They were, in the cabin of Junkers 88 D5-EV.

British nightfighters, Beaufighters and Mosquitos were fitted with another backward facing radar operating on the

Lichtenstein frequency, and sent out to join the bomber streams.

The equipment, 'Serrate' as it was codenamed, was hastily put together and the first operation with it was carried out on June 14th, just over a month after the Lichtenstein equipment had been delivered into the hands of the scientists, but it was successful. Five fighter planes went out with the bombers, each equipped with a 'Serrate' set, and they shot down one German nightfighter. The figures got better as the equipment was improved, and the fighter pilots gained confidence in using it.

They were the bait to attract the Germans, posing as limping bombers, trying to keep out of the main stream so as not to cause disruption when they revealed their hands, the Q-planes of the air. They allowed the German nightfighters to creep up behind them, then just before the German began his attack, and was committed to his course, the British nightfighter swung away, opened his own throttles and turned on to the tail of the enemy, reversing the roles.

By September 7th, 1943, two hundred and thirty-three sorties had been flown on thirty-four bombing nights; twenty-four German fighters had been attacked and thirteen destroyed in addition to one probable and five damaged.

There was yet another cause for disquiet among the German nightfighters. Their Lichtenstein sets could not differentiate between bomber and fighter. There was always the possibility that the 'sheep' that they were gleefully attacking could suddenly turn into a 'wolf'. This hazard was always there, although the German Junkers 88 nightfighter had a better performance than the Beaufighter VI aircraft being used for the 'Serrate' role then. When the Mosquito began to play the 'Serrate' game things became even more difficult for the Germans. The Mosquito was the plane that the Luftwaffe feared most of all. Plywood it was, but it had a performance that outstripped everything in the R.A.F. or the Luftwaffe.

CHAPTER TWENTY

INFILTRATING British nightfighters into the bomber streams became a successful tactic with Beaufighters. Between June and September 1943, Fighter Command's 141 Squadron sent them out on two hundred and twenty-three missions, lost three, but shot down thirteen German nightfighters, with another seven probably destroyed. It was even more successful, when, in November, 'Serrate' was taken seriously, special squadrons of 'Serrate' fighters were formed under 100 Group, and 141 Squadron was joined by 239 and 169 Squadrons – all equipped with Mosquito Mark IIs.

The odds against the German nightfighters mounted. In only a few months, since the Dyce landing in May, the dominant role of the German nightfighter over Germany had changed. From being the hunter, he was now the hunted. The feeling of confidence with which he had taken off in May had been replaced by one of resignation. Then, his only worry had been as to how many 'kills' he could add to his own and his squadron's totals. But by November, the news of Schmitt's defection, with the Lichtenstein Junkers, had percolated through the Luftwaffe. The radar advantage the nightfighters had over the British bombers had gone, and the Lichtenstein was now a disadvantage, enabling the British fighters to home in on them.

Every apparent bomber showing up on the Lichtenstein screen could, in fact, be a Mosquito, luring them into a trap. The Luftwaffe's confidence evaporated. It had been difficult enough to find the bombers through the screen of radar disturbance caused by 'Window' reflections, but now even that success, actually finding an aircraft, could lead to their own undoing.

Controllers on the ground told the fighter pilots that it should not be too difficult to find the bomber, despite 'Window'. Any radar blips on the radar screen which came close quickly should be ignored, it was obviously 'Window' dropping vertically. What the pilot had to look for was the blip which remained stationary, *that* was obviously an aircraft travelling at more or less the same speed as their own plane.

In practise it was different. The presence of a 'Window' cloud no longer meant that the British bombers were somewhere in the neighbourhood, for the high-flying Mosquitos had started dropping it too, a ruse to attract the nightfighters of the Luftwaffe within range. It caused what the Germans called a 'Mosquito panik' among their aircrews.

Harris' feint attacks confused the Germans completely. The bomber streams would be sent to one target, and a squadron of nightfighting Mosquitos to another, masquerading as a bomber stream. The German defences were split, and the Junkers sent to defend one town would find not bombers but Mosquitos waiting for them when they arrived. On one raid, in December when the Mosquitos made a feint attack on Dortmund, the German nightfighters who had been waiting fifteen minutes for the 'bombers' to arrive were attacked themselves by the Mosquitos and seven of them shot down. In one four-month period alone, three Squadrons of the German nightfighter force of some one hundred aircraft lost thirty-four planes and crews. No wonder that a 'Mosquito panik' existed.

The laconic descriptions which the Mosquito pilots gave of the nights 'trailing their coats' above Germany tell some of the drama. Flight Lieutenant Raby and his navigator Flight Sergeant Flint told the story of one of their successes in a report to their Intelligence officer.

'Mosquito took off West Raynham 2248 hours on a Serrate patrol in support of the bombers on Vierzon.

'Immediately after arrival at 4950N 0110E (presumed position of Beacon Biene) A.I. contact picked up at maximum range but disappeared at once. At 0100 hours while making ahead at maximum range and below crossing slowly port to starboard, as if contact was carrying out tight orbits of a beacon of which there were no visual indications. Mosquito tightened its starboard orbit and reduced height to twelve thousand feet coming in behind contact at eight thousand feet range. Contact reduced height to ten thousand feet and then straightened out making off in a southerly direction.

Mosquito also reduced height and closed in. A visual on the silhouette of a T.E. aircraft thought to be a range of two thousand, five hundred feet. As Mosquito closed in, the aircraft ahead suddenly throttled right back as if its pilot were aware of the presence of the Mosquito. Mosquito also throttled back and pulled the nose up, holding the visual at three hundred feet. The aircraft which was now positively identified as a Ju 88 of one of the latest marks, turned starboard with Mosquito following hard. Again it throttled back quickly and then turned starboard in its effort to shake off its pursuer, but Mosquito was a match for it and the visual was kept ahead at four hundred and fifty feet. At this point a regular series of either exhaust sparks or (more likely) tracer seen coming apparently from under enemy aircraft's nose and passing harmlessly over the top of the Mosquito which was now in a thirty degrees banking turn. In this position at a range of four hundred and fifty feet with the sights on enemy aircraft's fuselage, the pilot pressed the firing button and pulled the sight through to allow for between three-quarters and one ring deflection. The first burst, which was of about two seconds caused strikes all along the portside of the fuselage, the port wing and port engine and the latter burst into flames. At the same range another two-second burst of cannon was fired at enemy aircraft which was starting to roll over and go down. There was at once a violent explosion and enemy aircraft appeared to explode and blazing pieces flew back past Mosquito. Enemy aircraft was now well alight and going down steeply, but Mosquito followed it down firing altogether a further five brief bursts into the flames until it became impossible to follow it down vertically any further. As it went down enemy aircraft suddenly flared up into a flaming mass and there was a terrific explosion, the whole of the aircraft seemed to disintegrate. Both wings came off and they, with the fuselage all on fire, went separately down to the ground where it lit up the whole sky and burnt for about half an hour before one of the sections exploded anew.

This is claimed as a Ju 88 destroyed.'

There could have been little doubt about it. Flight Lieutenant Raby had more excitement that evening, for as he was completing that combat, another radar contact was picked up coming up fast behind him, but as the elevation control

142

of his radar had now gone u/s, he decided that 'Discretion would be the better part of valour, and Mosquito's nose was put hard down in a turning dive, straightening out suddenly at eight thousand feet doing three hundred miles per hour. The contact was then seen to pass out at maximum range well above.'

There were other Mosquitos about in the area to take care of that one.

'Serrate' missions produced their own fighter aces, as in all other forms of aerial warfare. One of them was Wing Commander J. R. D. Braham, D.S.O., D.F.C., A.F.C., C.D., who was responsible for nine out of the twenty-three victories of the Beaufighters in the early days when the secrets learned from the Lichtenstein Junkers were used against their inventors.

His very first mission in a stream of Lancasters and Halifaxes raiding the Ruhr brought him a success. He was one of six Beaufighters lurking among the bombers on the raid, scattered between ten thousand and eighteen thousand feet, and maintained his own height at twelve thousand feet, masquerading as a low-flying Halifax. His navigator, having got him to the target divided his time between the radar screens of their own radar and the 'Serrate', picking up the signals of a number of nightfighters as they moved in for what they thought were easy prey, and the bombers had been – until then.

After several nibbles which all petered out, Braham and his navigator got a bite. 'Bob, I've got another signal, turn gently to port,' the navigator instructed. Around them were three aircraft, in Braham's field of vision, all on fire, and as the bombers seldom shot down a nightfighter, he knew they all were British.

'Bob, I think this one is behind us. The signal is strong. Keep turning.'

The deadly game of hide and seek went on, the German nightfighter tracking on his Lichtenstein the plane in front, Braham allowing him to do so, but with his own navigator operator watching the enemy plane's movements until he decided that the time to strike had come. The German at last came within range, and he showed up on both the Lichtenstein screen and the plane's own radar.

'Bob, I've Aircraft Interception contact two thousand yards behind. Hard as possible port.'

'Are you sure it isn't one of our bombers?'

'Yes. It isn't. The Serrate and A.I. signals match up. Keep turning, he's only about one thousand yards and twenty degrees on your port and a little above. Now, ease the turn a little, and watch it. You're closing fast, you should see him in a second. He's only six hundred yards and well over to port.'

The roles had now been reversed, from hunting a bomber, the German nightfighter had now become the hunted, and he came into Braham's vision on his port beam. The Beaufighter's turn had taken him out of the narrow beam of the Lichtenstein's radar, and the German had lost the contact, But Braham hadn't. He recognized the shape of the Me 110, and eased behind him, opening fire at four hundred yards and easing the deflection on his electric gunsight so that the dot was centred on the Me's fuselage. Explosions appeared everywhere, and he dived towards the earth, crashing on the shore of the Zuider Zee.

The report that Flight Lieutenant D. Welfare and his navigator Flying Officer D. B. Bellis made after a mission from West Raynham was very brief – but it told it all. This time it was in a Mosquito.

'We crossed the coast at 0025 hours, ten minutes ahead of time and, nearing the patrol after seeing nothing at all, we got a contact astern crossing port to starboard at a range of fifteen thousand feet, height eighteen thousand feet. We got behind target and followed it through an orbit to port and a turn to starboard and down through three thousand feet. Indicated air speed was two hundred and sixty miles per hour and we closed in very slowly. At five thousand feet pilot obtained a visual during a turn to port and cutting off the turn, closed in to two thousand feet, identifying the target as an Me 110.

'Closed further smartly and gave a burst from two hundred feet. Aircraft was hit in port engine and along fuselage and blew up. Port wing was seen to drop off and aircraft went down in a spin in flames, hitting the ground with a big flash.

'We had another contact immediately behind us which peeled off when we got behind it. We then set course for base.

'Claim – One Me 110 destroyed.'

By June 1944, a year after the arrival of Schmitt and his crew had put the 'Serrate' weapon into the hands of Bomber Command, its use had become a science, and its results, gained from the reports of the crew were being studied by the Air Council. Groups of Mosquitos set off from West Raynham, and like Flying Officer Breithaupt and his navigator Flying Officer Kennedy, kept formation until a prearranged point above the enemy air defences was reached, when they split up and lay in wait. Their crossing had been observed by the Wurzburg radar down below, and the German night-fighters scrambled up to intercept the approaching group of bombers.

'The patrol as planned, was then started,' Breithaupt reported on his return. 'Mosquito broke formation and climbed slowly to fifteen thousand. At 9/10th, five hundred feet layer of cirro stratus straddled this precise altitude so Mosquito patrolled a line just North of and parallel to the Friesian Islands, immediately below a flat layer of cloud at one hundred and sixty-five miles per hour simulating a mine-layer.

'Obtaining no results with this procedure, we decided to lay ourselves open to direct and sudden attack by flying one hundred feet above the brilliantly moonlit clouds. Any enemy aircraft could have spotted us from extreme range – sil-houetted as we were directly above the beautifully white cloud layer.

'Nearing the extremity of our patrol, an A.I. contact was obtained hard to starboard at maximum range. To bring him in line ahead a hard turn of two hundred degrees was neces-sary. Range closed slowly to ten thousand feet when enemy aircraft turned one hundred and eighty degrees to port. This turn was followed and the range was closed to three thou-sand feet when a visual was obtained. Enemy aircraft was flying at quite a speed – two hundred and fifty miles per hour indicated at fifteen thousand, five hundred feet above clouds. We closed in to three hundred yards where enemy aircraft looked very much like a Beaufighter. Rather than make a mistake, Mosquito closed to about fifty feet behind and below (Quite safe as enemy aircraft was flying straight and level at the time – not having a notion of our presence). Black and white crosses were seen under the wings of the Ju

88 so we dropped back to one hundred yards and gave him a two-second burst. No more was needed as the port engine exploded and the blaze spread quickly enveloping fuselage and whole port wing. Ju 88 dived suddenly, then recovered and one person baled out, passing underneath our port wing.

'We followed it and gave it another burst for luck, but our cannons became inoperative for some obscure reason.

'Luckily we had settled the Ju 88's future with the first burst. Only the trimming was in control as it climbed, rounded off into a gentle dive, climbed steeply, dived steeply, climbed very steeply and dived vertically into the deck.

'Rest of patrol was uneventful and we landed at base at 0219 hours.'

'Serrate' became most effective when it was used in support of major bombing raids on targets in Germany, and the ratio of German fighters shot down was in the ratio of one to every eight completed 'Serrate' missions. The minor bombing raids, on industrial targets in the occupied countries didn't excite the German air defences quite so much. They were more interested in protecting their own country – so the minor raids were used to give the new 'Serrate' crews training experience. Even so, it brought a success rate of one to every eleven completed patrols.

The Air Ministry's Operational Research Section, which analysed the reports of 100 Group R.A.F. came to the conclusion that the success rate, great as it was, had far more benefits for the R.A.F. than were immediately apparent.

'It is suggested,' it told the Air Ministry, 'that the effectiveness of the high level Intruder operation must not be measured only in terms of enemy aircraft destroyed or damaged. There is also a considerable psychological effect on the enemy nightfighter crews. It is recommended that suitable propaganda be undertaken so that the enemy receives a very exaggerated picture of the number of this type of Intruder despatched.

'From the point of view of the effect of the operation on the enemy fighter strength, consideration of the enemy's probable production and wastage figures of enemy nightfighters suggest that he would be very seriously embarrassed by the loss of an additional fifty nightfighters per month. At the present standard of success, this would need a force of at

146

least eighty Serrate-type Intruders sent out on each major operation, but with new equipment such as A.I. Mk X, the number necessary may well be considerably reduced.'

Between them, Schmitt and Rosenberger had gone a long way to destroying the German air defences. The Operational Research Section's report dealing with the destruction of the Luftwaffe morale was already in operation, and the two men were already playing a large part in carrying out the Section's recommendations in their broadcasts to their former comrades. Bomber Command was now firmly in the driving seat in the skies over Germany.

CHAPTER TWENTY-ONE

WITH their screen of 'Window' to shield them, the R.A.F. were able to play tag with the German nightfighters since that first Hamburg raid of July 1943, able to laugh while the German radar controllers stormed, in impotent rage, at their inability to forecast where the next major bombing strike would be made. The strips of metallized paper were now as essential a part of a bomber's load as the bombs it carried. They were being used at the rate of three million bundles a month by everything that flew, at night, over Germany. To emphasize exactly *how* important 'Window' was, the Air Ministry was reminded by the Controller of Bomber operations in a memo on January 5th, 1945.

He gave some comparison figures.

Between the months of January to June 1943, before it was introduced, 8·8 per cent of bombers were damaged by anti-aircraft guns in raids on Germany. For the following six months, the figure was exactly halved. The German ground defences had been neutralized by it.

Prisoners of war, the Bomber Controller added, had revealed that the effect of 'Window' on the Lichtenstein equipment of the nightfighters was devastating. On many occasions, the nightfighters had actually returned to their bases because they thought their equipment had broken down. On the one occasion, a raid on Berlin in May, when the weather conditions had nullified the effect of the 'Window' screen, Bomber Command's losses had been exceptionally heavy.

The Air Ministry, which had been considering cutting down the amount of labour and materials needed to produce 'Window' was told by the Controller, 'Any restriction in the full use of "Window" will definitely result in a rise in our casualty rate, and there is no known alternative means of providing the protection normally afforded by this counter-measure.

'There is no question whatever that "Window" is an urgent and essential operational requirement, and all necessary steps should be taken as a matter of the highest urgency to ensure a full supply of "Window" material to Bomber Command in the German war, and the Strategic Air Forces in the Japanese war.'

Sir Arthur Harris, who had fought so hard to get the countermeasure introduced, was not going to have the lives of his bomber crews wasted, because the officials at the Air Ministry didn't realize how important it was.

General Schmidt, commanding the German night defences certainly did. Since taking over from the disgraced General Kammhuber, he had been forced to adopt entirely new tactics in an attempt to cope with the British bombers. Kammhuber had staked his reputation on a network of radar stations ringing the occupied countries and guarding the air approaches to Germany. Reichmarshall Goering had declaimed to an impressed German population, 'Anti-aircraft defences will be improved and better instruments installed. Nightfighters, which are at present stationed only in some parts of Germany, will gradually spread over the entire Reich, and then we shall talk again with England.'

He made a mistake in making that boast, for it told British Intelligence of his policy of extending the nightfighter system, and made them anxious to discover its secrets. By August 1943 they had done so. The system which Kammhuber had built up was laid bare by British Intelligence. A paper was even prepared on it and studied by the commanders of bomber units in the R.A.F.

Kammhuber had built up his Wurzburg radar stations over most parts of the north-western mainland of Europe. They were scattered about forty miles apart in Holland, north-western and northern Germany, and between forty and eighty miles apart on the Danish coast. These were Kammhuber's forward areas. Further inland, there was a great belt of stations stretching from Schleswig-Holstein, through north-west Germany, south-eastern Holland, eastern

149

Belgium and France, as far as the Swiss frontier – the Kamm-huber Line – at intervals of some twenty miles. And in accordance with Goering's declared policy, nightfighter areas had been established to guard important Target Areas within the Reich.

British Intelligence had learned this in various ways. It listened to the radio conversations of German nightfighters, picking up snippets of information which were fitted into the jigsaw Intelligence was compiling. In 1941, transmissions were heard on a wavelength which, from its pulse repetition rate, told the British scientists that it had a radar range of some twenty-five miles. The Photo Reconnaissance Unit planes were sent out to try and photograph an apparatus and given a rough area to search. In December 1941, the Unit got a photograph of a Wurzburg radar, which had to be the one with the twenty-five-mile range for which Intelligence had been looking. Then, from America, came a snapshot, taken by an Allied agent, of a strange piece of equipment poised on a tower in the Berlin Tiergarten. It was given to a Chinese scientist to study, and his report was that 'it was a large openwork paraboloid capable of rotation and elevation and used for Flak control. Its diameter was over twenty feet.' It was the Giant Wurzburg, the mainstay of the German ground radar system. There was no question of having agents bring even small parts of the Giant Wurzburg to Britain for study, it needed an expert to know what was important about it, but Intelligence and the R.A.F. *had* to know what the radar's capabilities were. The only way was to go and find out. So the Bruneval raid was launched, and the bits Britain needed stolen from the site itself. They gave the British the wavelength of the Wurzburg, and its range.

Information fed back from the Occupied countries had led British Intelligence to believe that the German nightfighter defences were split up into boxes with a forty mile radius. This was proved right in a radar duel, between a Beaufighter and a Junkers, off the Dutch island of Walcheren, at night. The British radar operators on the ground plotted the movements of both aircraft, and gave instructions to the Beaufighter, while the Giant Wurzburg operator did the same for the Junkers. It ended inconclusively when the two participants in the game of blindman's-buff strayed forty miles away from the coast. The Junkers turned back, obeying instructions from his ground control, who could no longer see him on their set. It gave the British the information they needed – the Giant Wurzburg's range was forty miles.

British spies in the occupied countries and in Germany were kept busy feeding back what information they garnered, to add to that which Oberleutnant Schmitt had been delivering through the grapevine controlled by his father, and which British Intelligence had gathered in a perfectly straightforward business fashion. Another German officer, highly placed in the Luftwaffe, found himself in financial trouble, and sold to the British a map of one area'which gave details of all the German searchlight positions. Added together, it told the S.I.S., and in turn Bomber Command, that there were two main areas to avoid when crossing the enemy coast, one along the coasts of Holland and the Bight, the other an inland belt running through north-west Germany, south-east Holland and eastern Belgium.

As Goering kept his promise, and built up his chain of Giant Wurzburg stations controlling the nightfighters inland, reports of the construction of these sites, with the house-sized gyrating paraboloid, and even snapshots of them, came back to the Intelligence office. One by one, the stations were plotted. The German Night Defences so painfully built up by General Kammhuber, and so carelessly given away by Reichsmarshall Goering, were complete, and were soon to be completely undone.

Sir Arthur Harris and his Bomber Command knew as much about the Kammhuber Line as Kammhuber did himself – except for one thing. There was still doubt as to whether the nightfighters of the Luftwaffe had an airborne radar. There had been suggestions, and reports from British agents which indicated they had. There had been vague descriptions of an aerial array on a twin-engined nightfighter, and so aircraft with listening devices on board were sent out to fly in areas where the German nightfighters operated. In December 1942, one of them tuned in to a wavelength of 61cms, heard a signal which grew in intensity right up to the moment it was attacked by a German nightfighter. The Luftwaffe *did* have an airborne radar.

There was no need to launch another Bruneval operation

this time however. The signal was sent back to Oberleutnant Schmitt. British Intelligence needed an example of the Lichtenstein radar. He decided that the best way was to take it over himself.

In July 1943, Goering's boast had turned back on him, the Kammhuber Line was broken, and so was General Kammhuber.

Yes, General Schmidt, his successor knew how important 'Window' was to Bomber Command, but there was nothing he could do about it. Over Germany his radar defences were jammed by it, and the forays of his fighters over the North Sea to meet the approaching bombers were hazardous once they approached the forty mile limit of the Giant Wurzburg radar screens. Their own Lichtenstein radar was jammed by 'Grocer' the ground transmitter set up at Dunwich specifically for that purpose.

'Grocer' had had a chequered career. Not until Schmitt, Rosenberger and Kantwill put their Ju 88 down at Dyce, had it been tested. Air Commodore M. G. F. Witty, the Director of Telecommunications was in charge of the project, and it was with some relief that he was able to write to Sir Sholto Douglas, the head of Fighter Command on June 18th, about testing 'Grocer' against the Ju 88.

'Due to lack of apparatus against which to test it, it has not been possible so far to determine the efficiency of the "Grocer" transmitter, and it is thus probable that full operational benefit is not being obtained from it by Bomber Command,' he wrote.

'As the necessary German equipment has now been obtained, it is proposed that tests of the "Grocer" transmitter shall be carried out as soon as possible, and I am therefore to request that Wing Commander Jackson of your Headquarters may be authorized to co-operate with Mr. Lees of T.R.E. (Technical Research Establishment) and to add this test to those on which he is already engaged.

'For the purpose of the test, the enemy equipment will be flown on a course between Farnborough and Boscombe Down, and the "Grocer" transmitter will be beamed in that direction. Arrangements are being made for a Wellington aircraft from 1473 Flight, which will be fitted with V.H.F. communication equipment, to be provided as a monitor aircraft, and to be used as the target aircraft if required.'

By then, Witty's experts had already been over the Junkers, examining the Lichtenstein, which had given them a lot of reassurance. One problem they had foreseen was that of covering a wide band of frequencies sufficiently well to jam each of them if the Germans could change their Lichtenstein speedily. But as the telecommunication experts found once they had been over Schmitt's plane, its construction was such that the frequency could certainly not be changed while the plane was in the air, and altering it on the ground would be a long and tedious business anyway. That was one problem they didn't have to solve.

But the first air test against the Wellington, with Squadron Leader Hartley at the controls of the Junkers, made up for it. It was a disaster. The intention was for the Wellington to fly in the 'Grocer' beam, and for the Junkers to intercept it with the aid of its Lichtenstein equipment, which they hoped would be jammed by the 'Grocer'. What happened was something of a farce. The improvized V.H.F. radio in the Wellington which was to keep it in touch with the Junkers broke down; a faulty valve in the 'Grocer' put that out of action, which didn't matter too much because the equivalent receiver in the Wellington also developed an intermittent fault, and no signals were received at all. And to round it off, the Wellington punctured a landing wheel so that a Spitfire had to be substituted as a target, but before any results could be assessed, the radar system was found to be u/s.

By February 1944, General 'Pepi' Schmidt had revised his nightfighter tactics, making the best of what defences were left to him, little more than the quality of the German planes and the courage of their pilots.

Unable to control his fighters from the ground, Schmidt used his heavily reinforced fighter defences on target interception. All the aircraft of a Geschwader operated as a group, with no limitation of the area of activity. The forty mile radius was abandoned, as the Wurzburg whose range it was was useless anyway. Instead, high-powered light and radio beacons were set up and used as assembly and waiting points. The fighters gathered around these beacons and waited for he bombers. The new method proved to be a success, but only a temporary one. The Bomber Command counter was to insert a few Mosquitos fitted with the 'Serrate' radar detector into the bomber streams.

Schmidt decided not to wait until the British bombers had actually arrived on their targets, but to intercept them on their way in. British bomber losses started to climb once more, and deep penetration raids into the heart of Germany could only be undertaken, at a heavy price once again. 'Bomber' Harris, always conscious of his losses used a confusion tactic, sending some bombers on deep raids into Germany, and others to attack the invasion targets in France, thus splitting the German air defences. Schmidt abandoned his radar stations, made useless by 'Window' and instead, made them aircraft reporting stations, whose job it was merely to pass on the approach of British bombers and their probable route, for the nightfighters to gather on the appropriate beacon. It also developed a new organization to intercept radar transmissions from the approaching bombers so that it could plot their route. Bomber Command retaliated by banning these transmission in areas where it would help the German Air Force more than the bombers themselves.

Then, on February 20th, 1944, the British played their first game of 'Spoof', and won it.

CHAPTER TWENTY-TWO

THE rules were very simple, but the Luftwaffe didn't know them. There were also a number of variations of the game, but again, Schmidt never knew which version it was that was being played against him. The first one was to send a group of pilots from an Operational Training Unit to make a sortie towards one of the more heavily defended targets in Germany – and then turn back just before reaching it, and being at risk. Even though the Germans waited until the last moment before taking off to meet the threat, it enabled a real mission to another target to escape relatively lightly.

An improvement on this was to add half a dozen heavy bombers to the unit of O.T.U. pilots, which carried on when the Training Unit's planes turned back for England. Instead of bombs, these bombers packed as much 'Window' as possible, which they dropped en route, and appeared to be a much greater force to the German radar than in reality. The German fighters concentrated on the 'Window' cloud, enabling the real force to slip in behind them, to the target.

A particularly effective variation was to put a few Mosquito fighters at the head of a force of bombers, armed with 'Window' on a spoof raid. Not only did it make the raid look more like a real one, as the bombers dropped their screens of 'Window' and blinded the German radar, it also increased the apprehension of the German fighters which, sent up to attack a large force of bombers, found themselves mixing it with Mosquitos. Then, just for a little more variety, Bomber Command would send a 'Window' raid out, bombers armed with 'Window', Mosquito fighters – and Mosquito bombers. The Germans, not knowing which hand to call, had tended to wait until bombs had actually been dropped before deciding when to send their fighters up and to which area. The Mosquito bombers dropped their relatively light loads, the Germans reacted and committed their fighters to that area – and the real bombing mission got through comparatively un-molested.

As in the early days of the 'Window' raids, when the German ground controllers at first celebrated what they thought were victories as the radar beams followed the falling 'Window' to earth , and then bewailed their inability to function, the spoof raids caused chaos. It took General Schmidt some time to work out counters to the new technique. In the mean-time, rival controllers in adjoining groups, gave running commentaries to their fighters based on guesswork, which were often completely contradictory.

On one occasion, the Jagddivisionen 1 Controller finally discovered that the target that night was Bochum, and ordered the fighters to make for that city, only to be con-tradicted by the Controller of Jagddivisionen 2, who had guessed the target to be Bremen, realized he was wrong, but was absolutely certain that it was *not* Bochum. By then, the raid on Bochum was over. But at Bremen, the fighters which the Controller of Jagddivisionen 2 had sent were fired on by their own Ack-Ack guns. One dropped a flare to illuminate the bombers for which he was seeking, which convinced the Jagddivisionen 2 Controller that the Pathfinders had arrived, and so, even while the Controller 1 was reporting that bombs were dropping on Bochum, and ordering all planes to the city, his opposite number was still countermanding the in-struction. Their mission accomplished, the British bombers left for home – the fighters still at Bremen one hundred and fifty miles away.

Because General Josef Schmidt decided to wait until the last possible second before committing his fighters, the full Luftwaffe effort did not arrive on a target city until between ten and fifteen minutes after the raid had started, by which time the earliest bombers would have left for home. To take full advantage of this time-lag, the bombers developed their 'concentrate in time' bombing, cutting the total length of the raid down to about twenty minutes, and giving the night-fighters still fewer targets from which to choose.

Schmidt's counter to this was 'route interception', even to the extent of directing fighters over the North Sea, hoping to catch the bombers, loaded with fuel and bombs, in the twilight. Changing his tactics caused Harris to alter those of

Bomber Command. Long roundabout routes to avoid the concentrations of German fighters were no longer popular, it gave the Germans more chances for an interception. The spoof raids fell into disfavour also, there was no point in hiding the target from the enemy.

The spoof had one more game to play however, the biggest and best of all. On the day of the invasion – D-Day.

Group Captain Leonard Cheshire was then the commander of 617 Squadron, the Dambusters, and he and his squadron were chosen for a special duty – to spoof the Germans into thinking that a convoy of ships, the invasion fleet, fourteen miles wide, was heading across the Channel to invade at Cap d'Antifer, while the real invasion fleet went for Le Havre.

The 617 Squadron and Stirlings from 018 Squadron were taken off operations for a month, instead they practised intricate flying, keeping precise speeds, times and heights for hours – eight hours in fact. They took it in turns. Eight aircraft flying a set distance apart, on predetermined courses at set speeds and heights throwing out 'Window' at set intervals. They flew thirty-five seconds on course, turned evenly, flew a reverse course for only thirty-two seconds before turning again back to the reverse course for another thirty-five seconds, again discharging 'Window'. Slowly, at a convoy's speed of seven knots, they would gradually cross the Channel towards Cap d'Antifer.

All the time, the first of the new bundle of 'Window' would leave the aircraft at the precise moment that the first of the previous bundle hit the water. The British scientists had worked the times out perfectly so that there was no interruption on the stream of blips picked up by the German coastal radar.

The training went on day and night, except for one day when the weather was bad, for a month. A steady two hundred miles per hour on a steady course and height, banking to retrace the route except for a vital three seconds, and then back again on to the original course.

It worked as the scientists had predicted. Cheshire's convoy droned on through the night of D-Day, flying at two hundred miles an hour, but approaching the French coast at no more than seven knots. German E-boats were sent in to attack it, the coastal artillery opened fire on it, and German infantry divisions were kept East of the Seine to defend against the expected invasion.

The weapon, whose use Heinrich Schmitt's defection had triggered off, had even helped in the invasion – another bundle of lives he and his crew had saved, as well as their own. Their erstwhile colleagues, however, were by now in desperate straits, unable even to take off or land on their own airfields without risking attention from marauding Mosquitos, used on Intruder operations. They circled the landing fields, waiting for the bare glimmer of light to which the Germans were by then reduced to assist in landing and take-off, and swooped down as soon as it came on.

The Mosquito, originally the Cinderella of the R.A.F., a plane that was designed and built despite the lack of interest shown by the Air Ministry, had become the dread of the Luftwaffe. Apart from its 'Window' scattering role in real and spoof bombing attacks, Air Vice-Marshal Donald Bennett, leader of the Pathfinder force had realized it was the ideal plane for the new role he was given.

To make the concentration of bombing even more effective, 'Bomber' Harris skimmed his squadrons of the best pilots and navigators, to send them ahead to mark the targets to be bombed, so that the following force of Lancasters would know exactly where to drop their loads. He gave the job of forming the new arm to Bennett, with the latest radar and radio equipment, and 'Oboe', a device controlled from the ground which told the bomber when it was over its target.

Bennett found that a small order of bomber Mosquitos, with a bomb bay just big enough to take a five hundred pound target indicator had been placed by the Ministry of Aircraft Production, but no-one seemed to know what to do with them. He took the little plane up on test flights by day and night, and found that it was exactly what he wanted. He had to convince the Air Ministry and Bomber Command itself however, who argued that the wooden plane, frailly built and without any armament would be shot down before it could fulfil its mission.

To try to divert the bombers, and save the actual cities, General Schmidt had started using the British techniques of deception, and when raids were expected would create dummy towns, surrounded by searchlights and Ack-Ack which 'defended' violently as the bombing force crossed it. Dummy incendiaries were even let off to make it look as if the 'town' – in reality open fields – was already under bomber attack. Many bombers were deceived and dropped their bombs harmlessly. The Pathfinder force put an end to that ruse.

The Mosquitos went in fast, dropped the Target Indicators, which burst by barometric pressure at about two hundred feet from the ground and cascaded a large number of coloured pyrotechnic candles, each burning for only a short duration, and being replenished by another drop, so that the German firefighters' task of dousing them was made impossible. With the target area well lit up and defined, the Lancasters made no mistake.

Once Bennett had proved the virtues of the Mosquito as a bomber, its services were called on more and more for special operations that required speed and delicacy, and where saturation and heavy bomb loads were not necessary. Raids like the one which killed a lot of Gestapo, destroyed their records and released Danish resistance fighters from the Gestapo headquarters in Copenhagen. It had to be a pinpoint operation, the slightest error would cause the death of a lot of Danish people. The target was just one building in the centre of Copenhagen – Shell House, a block of offices that the Gestapo had turned into their headquarters and prison. Air Chief Marshal Sir Basil Embry who planned the operation had a model built of the target area so that the route towards the target could be demonstrated to the pilots and bomb-aimers. In one wing of the offices a large number of resistance fighters were imprisoned, and were almost certain to be killed in the raid, but the Danes were prepared to accept that near certainty. They preferred to die at the hands of the British bombers rather than those of the Gestapo. A house near the target was also certain to be damaged, but the Danes were philosophical about that too – it was a brothel used by the Germans, and if a bomb hit that by accident, no-one would worry. What was important was that the raid took place, that the Gestapo records were destroyed before the Germans acted upon them, and wiped out the Danish resistance movement.

Embry used eighteen Mosquitos for the attack, flying himself as number three in the formation, at fifty feet above the North Sea, and low over Denmark, pulling up to avoid high-tension cables and trees, flying parallel to the ground well below tree-top level.

The Mosquitos attacked Shell House at below roof-top level, down the main thoroughfare, aiming their bombs directly at the target. The raid was not without tragedy though. One Mosquito hit the upright of a bridge, and crashed on a convent school. The second wave of Mosquitos, thinking this scene of devastation was the target, dropped their bombs on the wreckage, killing many Danish children. Three Mosquitos and an escorting Mustang fighter were lost – but the Gestapo headquarters and its records were destroyed, twenty-six Gestapo killed, and all the Danish prisoners liberated without one being killed. The Danes accepted the loss of their children as part of the price of war, and described the raid as a victory.

The speed and manoeuvrability of the Mosquito was even greater when used as a fighter and nightfighter, and even though the Germans had designed their own 'Serrate'-type radar, which gave a signal when they were in the beam of an approaching Mosquito fighter, 'Naxos', as a fighting aircraft, they were outmatched.

The 'Naxos' was the only defence left to the German nightfighters and their ground control. Before taking off, the ground control would sweep the sky, searching for what it knew was there, a lurking Mosquito. When it was as clear as it was likely to be, a green light was flashed at the Junkers or Messerschmitt which would dash into the air, followed by the others in the flight. If they were lucky, they would get a shouted instruction from one of the operators just before take-off, giving them the latest position of the bomber stream they were to attack. But often, they were replaced by a loud-speaker warning from the operations room, warning that the Mosquitos would be overhead in seconds, urging the night-fighters into the air right away, or risk being bombed.

It required split-second timing, as the nightfighter opened the throttles of his engines, and held the plane back with the brakes, the flare-path lights were switched on, and switched off again as soon as the plane leaped into the air.

Wilhelm Johnen, still flying in the closing days of the war, having survived so many missions, described one such encounter.

'I taxied in the dark and took up my place on the runway. After a brief glance at the instruments and the engines I gave her full throttle. The flarepath lights went on and were switched off as soon as I was airborne. I had hardly levelled out the machine when Mahle shouted, "Look out, Mosquito."

'I thought as much. The Tommies had waited until the fish was on the line, but I did not intend to make things easy for them. I hedge-hopped over the fields and shook off my pursuer. The British were very tough but they did not propose to indulge in any near the ground aerobatics. My crew breathed with relief. We'd made it. We all felt rather uncomfortable after this display of stunting. I zoomed and forced the engines to take me up to twelve thousand feet. On the tactical waves we heard new enemy reports. Suddenly there was decisive news.

' "Achtung, achtung. Bombers are flying in the direction of Nuremburg. A moderate-sized formation reported over the Ulm making for Wurzburg. Probable objectives Nuremburg and Wurzburg."

' "They're not even going to respect the hospital city of Wurzburg," growled Mahle. "There really aren't any armament factories there."

'I thought for a moment, Wurzburg or Nuremburg. I decided for the former and changed on to a northerly course. The night was reasonably clear apart from a few regulation clouds at nine thousand feet. "We might be able to use them if a Mosquito gets on our tail," said Mahle. The moon treacherously lit up the great river. Grasshof reported contacts on his radar. Then the storm broke. We were approaching the bombers. Before we had got to the enemy, the Pathfinders had dropped their marker flares over the city. Parachute flares drifted down making the night look ghostly. "Courier eight hundred yards ahead," reported Grasshof.

'At that moment, a slight ticking began in my headphones. Long-range nightfighters! Despite this warning I remained on my course and gave the Messerschmitt full throttle. The ticking grew louder. "Mosquitos," shouted Mahle.

'I took avoiding action. The British pilot's tracers went wide below my right wing. The hunt started again. Now we were flying directly over the city among the bomber stream.

'Then the appalling destruction began. On the orders of the Pathfinders, the four-engine bomber crews opened their bays and rained incendiaries on to the city below. The phosphorus ignited as soon as it hit the air and joined into a huge burning cloud which slowly settled on the city. It was a Dantesque and terrible sight. Those unfortunate people who were still in the city! This fiery cloud knew no pity. It sank on churches and houses, palaces and citadels, broad avenues and narrow streets. At the outset, burning drops spurted from the cloud causing isolated fires. Then the burning veil enveloped Wurzburg. In a few moments a gigantic patch of flame lit up the dark night and turned the clouds to scarlet. Wurzburg was burning. By the glow of the doomed city the bombers found their direction. The small wings and slender bodies gleamed brightly. I could have shot time and time again, but as soon as I was in position Mahle shouted, "Achtung! Mosquito!" I had instructed him only to warn me in case of great danger. Thus I dared not reflect when his words rang out. The delay of a second and we should fall like a blazing torch out of the sky.'

Then Johnen was given the opportunity Schmitt had so steadfastly resisted in *his* days as a Luftwaffe nightfighter. A Lancaster crossed his path.

'Without a thought, I poured a long burst into its fuselage and wings. The crate exploded in the air and spun down with its crew. That was my only kill over Wurzburg and my last kill of the war. It attracted the entire enemy nightfighter pack on my heels. We could hardly watch the bomber crash on the ground before they set about us. The "Naxos" apparatus lit up constantly. Mahle no longer shouted "Achtung!" but sat and fired his tracers at the Mosquitos. No avoiding action, no banking, no hide and seek in the clouds was of any avail.

'The British pilot remained on my tail. Fortunately he always began from long range and his aim was inaccurate.

'And then suddenly Mahle shouted in terror, "Mosquito close behind us."

'His voice made me shudder. Even as I banked the burst hit my machine. There was a reek of smoke and fire. Terrify-

162

ing seconds ahead, but I let my machine dive to be rid of my pursuer. The altimeter fell rapidly – 2,500 ... 2,000 ... 1,500 ... 1,000. Now I had to pull out unless I wanted to go straight into the ground. I pulled with all my might on the joystick and got the diving machine under control. Luckily the controls answered. There was still an acrid smell of smoke in the cabin. Perhaps a cable was smouldering, but the engines were running smoothly.

'We hedge-hopped over Swabia towards our airfield in Leipheim. Mahle lit up the cockpit with his torch. Everything was in order. Then he focused it on the engines. There was a white trickle on the starboard wing. Petrol! One of the pipes had been shot through and the fuel was leaking out. The needle on the fuel indicator slowly sank to empty. This was a fatal situation. But misfortunes never come singly. Mahle reported reactions in the "Naxos", and the sinister ticking started again in the headphones. The British never give up. This one pursued us even to our airfield. We had to land and avoiding action was impossible. It was pointless coming down anywhere except in Leipheim. Grasshof called the airfield which replied faintly. A few terrifying minutes ... I pumped petrol from the port into the starboard tank with the electric pump. Would we have enough?

'If the right engine conked it would be the end. I now spoke to the ground station myself. Everything depended upon a skilful landing or else the Mosquito would shoot me down as I approached the runway.

' "Lobster from Thrust 1. Come in please."

' "Thrust 1 from Lobster. Victor, victor. Loud and clear. Take care – nightfighters circling the airfield."

'That was to have been expected. The Britisher did not want to miss me.

'I replied, "Victor, victor. I must land. Little fuel left. Don't light up. I'll land blind. Put a white lamp on the landing across and one red lamp at the end of the flare-path. Don't switch on."

'The ground station had understood my plan to fool the Mosquito. Mahle sat at his guns in the rear cockpit. I lowered the wing flaps to twenty degrees and circled at low speed over the airfield. The British were searching. The ticking in my headphones was continuous but the fellows did not dare to come down. I was no more than one hundred feet above the ground. Tensely I watched the proceedings on the runway. At any moment the two ground lights would go on. The perspiration was pouring from my forehead. I only hoped that the two lights would be sufficient to bring my machine down in safety. I must rely entirely upon my instruments, for the two petrol lamps would neither give me my height nor the direction of the machine. Should I not let them turn the lights on just as I landed? But this seemed too risky. The Mosquitos were looking with Argus eyes at this field, and if it lit up they would immediately see the machines parked and the sheds. During these reflections I gained height. The red control lamps of the petrol tanks lit up. That meant fuel for not more than five minutes. I must land . . .

'I had tuned in my radio to the ground station in order to give the Tommies no hint. But now I was in great danger. I pressed the button.

' "Lobster from Thrust 1. Hurry, please, hurry please, fuel for another five minutes."

'Oberfeldwebel Kramer replied at once. "Thrust 1 from Lobster. Lamps in position. You can land." We looked for them and Mahle was the first to discover them. They gave a very faint light. Directly above the white lamp I started the stopwatch and set my machine on its course. The white light disappeared behind the tail unit. If I flew correctly as I came in over the field it would bob up ahead of me.

'Mahle suddenly shouted : "There's one ahead to starboard. A bit higher."

'I only caught a glimpse of exhaust pipes disappearing in the darkness. "For God's sake don't shout so loud, Mahle."

'The seconds passed. If only my fuel would last out. A short pressure on the hydraulic gear. Undercarriage lowered . . . At any moment now the white lamp would appear in the darkness. My eyes peered into the night. There it was. Throttle back. Float . . . The wheels touched down. I put on the brakes and the machine gently came to a standstill. We'd made it. Grasshof opened the cockpit roof.

' "Herr Hauptmann, the Tommies are droning right overhead. Something's up."

'I cautiously gave a little throttle to prevent the flames darting from the engine. Any reflection would betray us. In the darkness we taxied to our dispersal pen. Then the accident happened. An over-eager mechanic, trying to be helpful, flashed his green torch. The Mosquitos were on the watch. I turned the machine into the wind and cut off the engine.'

That *was* Hauptmann Johnen's last kill. Even as he and his crew leapt from their Messerschmitt, the Mosquito which had made the duel a vengeance mission swooped down, and destroyed it.

CHAPTER TWENTY-THREE

A FIGHTER destroyed on the ground was just as dead as one shot down in the air, but it wasn't the same. For one thing, the pilot probably escaped, and the destruction of the aircraft was not as complete as one that ploughed into the ground, from a height. But the constant harassment of German night-fighters in operation 'Flower', the code-name given to the Intruder operation over the nightfighter dromes not only wore at the nerves of the pilots, tiring them and making them more liable to errors of judgement, they produced a useful dividend in aircraft destroyed. In one period, in early 1944, for the loss of five British Mosquitos, twenty-four German aircraft were destroyed and another twenty damaged, a success rate of $9 \cdot 1\frac{1}{2}$ per cent of the sorties sent out.

'Serrate', where the Mosquitos 'trailed their coats', posing as bombers and letting the nightfighters of the Luftwaffe get on their tails before revealing their hands was more success-ful – and more dangerous. In the same period, there were seven hundred and sixty sorties, which cost twenty-four Mos-quitos and their crews. But fifty-one German planes were totally destroyed, shot down from the air, and seven dam-aged. In the year since Schmitt had handed over his Junkers, its Lichtenstein had been stripped down, and the counter-measure to it, 'Serrate', invented. The German air defences had been reduced from an integral, cohesive force, to one of individual freelance operations, loosely controlled from the ground by a running commentary given by controllers who could only guess at the targets the bombers were aiming for, and whose commentaries anyway were more often than not jammed by the bombers themselves.

Taking off was a hazard itself, each drome was watched from above by 'Flower' Mosquitos, and it got to the stage when the Flight Control operator would ring up the fighter dispersal to announce that 'the duty intruder has arrived'.

166

The pilots assumed that there would be a Mosquito above them, waiting for them to get into the air, and taking off was a long, low-flying business, waiting for the clicking of the 'Naxos' to start as they gained height, and tried for the bomber streams where a 'Serrate' equipped Mosquito could well be waiting to lead them into the trap of a table-turned attack.

Landing was delayed as long as possible, for the pilots knew that by then they would be tired, their eyes having spent hours straining through the night skies for the sight of a Lancaster's exhausts, their ears tuned for the clicking of the 'Naxos', and they still had to run the gauntlet of the Intruders circling their dromes.

They would leave it to the last minute before deciding on which of the alternative airfields to put their planes down, learning in brief snatches of conversation over the V.H.F. radio which one had the least Intruder activity. Tired as they were, they had to come down to one hundred and fifty feet or lower, and approach the landing-strip into the wind, for only at that height could the cowled landing lights be seen. If there were too many Mosquitos watching for him, the lights on a nearby field would be switched on to attract the Intruders away, so that he could slip into the field they had abandoned. Sometimes it worked, sometimes two Mosquitos would be on patrol, and one would stay behind. Then it didn't. At the beginning of 'Operation Flower', red flashing lights would be lit, and fireworks let off to warn the Me 110s and Ju 88s that a Mosquito was lurking in the air. But by the end of 1944, they didn't bother to give any warning. It was assumed that there would always be an Intruder waiting for the German planes to land.

The only answer the Luftwaffe found to the Mosquito, the plane the Air Ministry didn't really want, but which made its name in the 'Window' and 'Serrate' operations, using the secrets found in the Lichtenstein apparatus against the Germans who designed it, were jet fighters.

The Mosquitos had a clear run over wherever they wanted to fly in Germany, too fast and too manoeuvrable for the Mes and Jus to catch, whether on bombing operations or just playing havoc with 'Window'. Berlin was well within their range after the invasion, and the Mosquito raids drove Hitler into a fury and Goering into a panic as a result.

He called in one of Germany's best pilots, Oberleutnant Welter, who had been test-flying planes as they came off the assembly line, and detailed him to find some way of curbing the Mosquitos. He tried the Messerschmitt 109 and Focke Wulf 190 in their latest versions, but even with superchargers, neither could catch the Mossy. They tried fitting water injection and even ice injection to the Focke Wulfs, but while they increased the speed, they also damaged the engines. The only hope, Welter told Goering, was in jet planes, and he was given the decision to choose between the Arado 234 or the Messerschmitt 262 then undergoing trials.

He tried both, and managed to catch and shoot down a Mosquito with the Me 262 in September, when it was caught in the searchlights over Berlin.

He opted for the Me 262, and asked for a two-seater to be built with a new Air Interception radar. But it was March 1945 before the plane Welter wanted went into operations, and had only three Mosquitos to its credit when the war ended. However, Welter was convinced that the jet Me would have driven the Mosquito out of the air, and when VE-Day came, the plans were in being to form Squadrons of the jets. But Welter didn't know about the British jet-fighters.

CHAPTER TWENTY-FOUR

OF the six men so closely involved with the events following the landing of the Ju 88 at Dyce in 1943, three have scored and three have not. Their parts played, the three Germans, Heinrich Schmitt, Paul Rosenberger and Erich Kantwill vanished into the wings, and into the obscurity they sought. Schmitt *had* succeeded in his objective, to bring the war more speedily to an end and overthrow the Nazi Government. His father too, lived to see the return of the Social Democrats to power in Germany, although he was too old by then to play any further part in the administration of the country. But the crew of the Junkers knew that, though protected by the British and Allied occupation forces, their presence would not be welcome to their former comrades if their identity was known.

They were given pensions by the British Government, but that of Kantwill, who remained a Nazi, never more so than when he found himself in Britain, friendless, and refusing to co-operate as did Schmitt and Rosenberger, in broadcasting appeals to his former comrades to surrender, was less than the other two. It continued for some little while after the war ended, but Kantwill by 1948 had to re-establish his own way in civilian life. He became a waiter, and then a flower seller, always at odds with his conscience. In 1950 he returned to Dortmund and to Anneliese, the wife he had left behind on May 9th, 1943, and his daughter, but things had changed. There was nothing left between them, and he admitted that things hadn't turned out the way he thought they would. He wrote a plaintive letter to his daughter in 1951, from Canada, asking her to remember him with love, and then crossed the border into America where he has succeeded in losing himself.

Paul Rosenberger, the radio operator, who used the name Obermeyer, during his broadcasts on the radio station operating from London, 'Gustav Siegfried Eins' also returned to Germany for a visit, and also visited his wife. But he is now divorced from her, and has established a new life and identity for himself in France.

Heinrich Schmitt still remains the enigma of the three. He returned to Germany, and flying, when the war ended, using his own name and is married with two children. The Social Democrats whose cause he did so much for, found him work as a pilot with a German industrial organization, and his salary, plus his British pension enabled him to retire at the age of sixty and leave Bonn, for a new country where the events of May 9th, 1943, no longer matter. He gave one interview before leaving Germany, to Gunther Stiller, of the German newspaper Bild am Sonntag, and made it clear that, like Rosenberger, he regretted nothing.

'My father was a long-standing enemy of National Socialism,' he said. He was the secretary to Gustav Stresemann, the Foreign Minister of the Weimar Republic, and he had kept in touch with the Social Democrats who escaped to Prague, Paris and London, and formed part of the circle around Erich Ollenhauer who was from 1952 until 1963 the chairman of the Social Democratic Party. He and Fritz Heine, the Speaker of the Social Democratic Party set up a base in London during the war and continued the campaign against Hitler from there. The leader there was Hans Vogel, and they formed a Government ready to establish democracy in Germany as soon as the war was over.

'My part in it was a minor one, to act as the link between Britain and the homeland.'

Schmitt's link, however, was more than a minor one, for he admitted that the landing at Dyce in 1943, was not the first time he put a Luftwaffe plane down on an English airfield during the war.

No records of the landing exist on the files of R.A.F. Lincoln, but, said Schmitt, he delivered a package to a waiting R.A.F. officer in a Dornier 217, on the night of May 20th, 1941, just ten days after Rudolf Hess, Hitler's deputy, bailed out of his Me 110 over Scotland.

'It was all part of the grey war that existed at that time,' said Schmitt. 'I wasn't the only German pilot to land, by arrangement in Britain, and several British pilots made land-

170

ings in Germany, which were known to the people who mattered on our side. It was well-known that Hitler was prepared to pay a high price to make peace with Britain, and the secret flights only ended when we attacked Russia, and Britain and Russia became allies.'

That landing was an official one, on behalf of the Luftwaffe, and what the package was, Schmitt never knew. His second landing at Dyce was on behalf of the R.A.F. and he knew well what the effects of that would be, but, he said, he would do it again. He made the right choice.

'I saved many lives. I sent many messages through my father in Thuringia which enabled Social Democrats like himself, and Jews, to escape out of Germany through Paris, Spain, Lisbon into safety.

'I knew that handing over my plane and its secrets would cost the lives of a lot of my comrades in the Luftwaffe, but the Nazis were never prim. Hitler would have seen Germany die to the last man, as he showed ultimately. He placed all his eggs in one basket. So did we.

'When my plane was shot-up over England in May 1942 and my flight-mechanic seriously injured and Rosenberger slightly injured, I could have surrendered then and become a prisoner of war. It wasn't easy flying it back with one engine, but I didn't want to arrive as a PoW, but voluntarily. Certain officers of my unit had become suspicious of me, but they concluded then that I was O.K. so I was able to continue working for the British for another year.

'We wanted to give more political weight and influence to the Social Democrats in England on the British post-war policy towards Germany. It didn't quite work out that way, but I think it had some influence on the British attitude after the war.

'Our Government in exile wanted to do all it could to end the war as quickly as possible and build a new Germany. I had seen enough with my own eyes how things stood for us. The oppression, the deaths on the battlefields, the murder of my Jewish fiancée. The country was wading in blood. It was enough.'

Of the three Britons, Dr. R. V. Jones, as he then was, played the roles of many men during the war. A scientist, the inventor of 'Window', he was then the Assistant Director of Intelligence of the R.A.F. and became the Director in 1946. He is still a consultant to the Ministry of Defence and has held every scientific post in the British Government that is worth holding. He is now the Professor of Natural Philosophy at the University of Aberdeen, a C.B., C.B.E., and F.R.S. in addition to many foreign honours.

Wing Commander Derek Ainslie Jackson, O.B.E., D.F.C., A.F.C., M.A., D.Sc., Legion of Merit (U.S.A.), Chevalier, Legion d'Honneur, France, is also a Professor in Paris where he now lives with his fourth wife.

Squadron Leader Christopher Hartley is now Air Marshal Sir Christopher Hartley, K.C.B., C.B., C.B.E., O.B.E., D.F.C., A.F.C., B.A. He is the deputy chairman of the British Hovercraft Corporation and lives on the Isle of Wight.

THE END

633 SQUADRON BY FREDERICK E. SMITH

This was the mission on which the success of Operation Overlord –
the invasion of Europe – depended. The chosen squadron was No.
633 whose pilots flew with skill and daring.

Their target was a fjord in Norway, where the Germans were
known to be developing something so secret, that not even the
crews of the Mosquitoes which were to fly on the mission could be
told about it. They knew it was a dangerous mission, but they
could not know just how dangerous it would turn out to be.

0 552 08169 8   75p

633 SQUADRON: OPERATION RHINE MAIDEN
BY FREDERICK E. SMITH

After the near-suicide mission to the Swartfjord, which had
claimed so many lives, morale among what was left of 633 Squadron was at its lowest ebb. Unbearable tension, stupid wrangling
among the survivors and problems with replacement recruits were
tearing the squadron apart . . .

The new Commander, Ian Moore – young, brilliant and
determined – knew that the only thing that would pull it together
again was the challenge of another vital mission . . .

The Germans were developing a new anti-aircraft rocket, code
name Rhine Maiden, which posed the most deadly threat so far to
the Allies' invasion plans. So the top brass decided that 633
Squadron should first flatten the rocket factory on a bombing run,
and then make a daring strike on an underground target buried
deep in a Bavarian valley – in broad daylight . . .

0 552 10155 9   85p

FIVE ROADS TO FREEDOM BY GEORGE BEESON

'IF YOU CAN'T DIG YOUR WAY OUT, KID YOUR WAY OUT AND IF THAT FAILS THINK AGAIN ...'

George Beeson was a genius among escapers in the Second World War. A Sergeant in the R.A.S.C., he was captured and taken prisoner in 1940. After a gruelling forced-march into Poland, without medical aid (he had been wounded) and with the absolute minimum of barely edible food, he arrived at Poznan P.O.W. camp. From there on, he occupied himself with escaping. In all he made five separate attempts and finally got away.

With modesty and humour, the author describes the horrors of the eastern camps, the long battle of wits with his later captors and his extraordinary adventures with the French Resistance. The result is an enthralling and deeply moving book.

0 552 10714 X   70p

GREEN BEACH BY JAMES LEASOR

One man – one mission . . . and one of the greatest true stories of courage during World War II.

On the 19th August 1942 six thousand Canadian and British commandos strike at Hitler's Europe. With them is one young man – a man whose mission is so vital that he cannot possibly be allowed to fall into enemy hands . . . alive.

'GREEN BEACH has blown the lid off one of the Second World War's best-kept secrets'.—*The Daily Express.*

0 552 10245 8   75p

REIGN OF HELL BY SVEN HASSEL

Burning, looting, raping, murdering, Hitler's Penal Regiments advanced on the centre of Warsaw leaving in their wake a bloody trail of death and destruction. They killed indiscriminately. Pole or German; young or old; man, woman, child – anyone who crossed their path was eliminated. For Himmler had sworn that Warsaw would be razed to the ground – if it took every member of the German army to do it! And against the Fuhrer's expendable battalions, for whom life had no meaning, the battle for Warsaw became an inferno – an endless reign of hell . . .

0 552 09178 2   95p

SS GENERAL BY SVEN HASSEL

The 27th Panzers in Hitler's Penal Regiment had fought through the winter in the hell-hole that was Stalingrad. Now there were few survivors from the last massive Russian attack. Weary and nauseated by the horrors they'd seen on the Russian front they crawled into a bunker near the banks of the Volga. Hunger, they had discovered was more demoralizing than fear or defeat. Then the brutal SS general arrived . . .

0 552 08874 9   95p

A SELECTED LIST OF
WAR BOOKS PUBLISHED BY
CORGI

☐	10889 8	Holocaust	*Gerald Green* £1.25
☐	10400 0	The Bloody Road to Death	*Sven Hassel* 95p
☐	09761 6	Blitzfreeze	*Sven Hassel* 95p
☐	09178 2	Reign of Hell	*Sven Hassel* 95p
☐	08874 9	SS General	*Sven Hassel* 95p
☐	08779 3	Assignment Gestapo	*Sven Hassel* 95p
☐	08603 7	Liquidate Paris	*Sven Hassel* 95p
☐	08528 6	March Battalion	*Sven Hassel* 85p
☐	08168 x	Monte Casino	*Sven Hassel* 85p
☐	07871 9	Comrades of War	*Sven Hassel* 95p
☐	07242 7	Wheels of Terror	*Sven Hassel* 95p
☐	07241 9	Legion of the Damned	*Sven Hassel* 95p
☐	10343 8	Cross of Iron	*Willi Heinrich* 75p
☐	09485 4	The Savage Montain	*Willi Heinrich* 65p
☐	10393 4	The Blue Max	*Jack D. Hunter* 75p
☐	08371 2	The Dirty Dozen	*E. M. Nathanson* £1.25
☐	10300 4	The Scourge of the Swastika	*Lord Russell of Liverpool* 85p
☐	10301 2	The Knights of Bushido	*Lord Russell of Liverpool* 85p
☐	10741 7	633 Squadron: Operation Crucible	*Frederick E. Smith* 80p
☐	10155 9	633 Squadron: Operation Rhine Maiden	*Frederick E. Smith* 85p
☐	08169 8	633 Squadron	*Frederick E. Smith* 75p

All these books are available at your bookshop or newsagent, or can be ordered direct from the publisher. Just tick the titles you want and fill in the form below.

....

NAME (Block letters) ....

ADDRESS ....

....